The Farme

By

Robin Armstrong Brown

With Illustrations

By

Penny Martin

The sun had set on yonder hill, across the cloudy moor,
When, weary and lame, a boy there came up to a farmer's door.
Can you tell me, if here there be a man who'll me employ
To plough and sow, and reap and mow, and be a farmer's boy,
And be a farmer's boy?

West country song - traditional.

For Rosemary, Penny, and Patrick,

who were there.

For Di, who encouraged and supported

me during the writing of this book.

And in fond memory of

Mary and Bill Armstrong Brown.

Acknowledgements

I wish to especially thank Penny Martin, my sister, for joining forces with me in the production of this book. She has done all of the illustrations, working from life, from memory, from sketches and old photographs, to bring the text to visual life in a truthful and touching way. The Old Farm, and the Sussex countryside, was her home as it was mine. Penny and my other sister Rosemary between them supplied a part of the story that I had never known, and gave me a fitting way of bringing the tale to a close.

I must give personal thanks and great credit to Ian Hampson of Champion Design; not only both for his enormous patience and creative ideas on editing and use of fonts, but especially for many long hours of sensitive work in mounting the illustrations to add the greatest effect to the text. Thanks are also due to my wife Diana, and my daughter Sue Armstrong Brown, for their care in editing and proof reading the manuscripts.

Finally, and most sincerely, I wish to thank Di for her support and endless patience during the writing of this book, particularly during the later chapters. It was not easy to relive those last years at the farm: I know I was pre-occupied and moody. Her encouragement saw me through.

Printed by Lulu UK
www.lulu.com/gb

Introduction

I closed my book - 'Let's not go to the Dogs Tonight', by Alexandra Fuller. It was the shattering story of a White Farmer's daughter growing up in post-colonial Africa. And I thought 'I too have a story to tell'. I grew up on a farm in East Sussex. During the early part of Hitler's War the Luftwaffe were constant visitors, as were the Doodlebugs later. Our part of England was essentially occupied territory, with the difference that it was occupied by our own troops. The war was the background of our lives till I was seven years old. Rural Sussex was my home, until I was sent to boarding school on the coast. But in parallel with my teenage years, a story was growing that cast an ever-lengthening shadow on our lives, until it swallowed them completely. I put down Alexandra's book, went to the table, and started to write.

In telling this story I had a problem that is more common in fiction than in autobiography. How could I tell a story through the eyes of the youth that was me, and still give the background that my father knew, but from which he wanted to shelter his family? And then lead to a treacherous truth, which even my father did not believe until it was too late? My sister had kept an old box of my father's papers. In there I found his story, written in his own words in a legal deposition. Rather than use the facts which he alone knew, in my story and in my voice, I have chosen to use a different font, and to tell his story in his own words. In just a few places I have synthesised a paragraph out of different documents, and once only I have summarised the larger picture using his voice.

Readers may have difficulty in believing that public servants could behave as depicted here. I can only assure them that I, and my sisters and brother, saw this happening with our own eyes. Certain names have been altered, in order to have the necessary freedom to tell the truth. This is the tale of a Sussex Paradise Lost.

2 December 2008

Part 1
Child of the Weald

Part 2
Son of the Downs

The Old Farm

Part 1

Child of the Weald

God gave all men all earth to love,
But, since our hearts are small,
Ordained for each one spot should prove
Beloved over all:
That, as He watched Creation's birth,
So we, in god-like mood,
May of our love create our earth
And see that it is good.

Sussex. Rudyard Kipling

The Old Farm

It is early on a winter morning, the sky is still a dark blue, and a waning half-moon is hanging in the sky over the oast house. Under the kitchen window, looking out with his nose pressed hard against the little pane in the bottom corner, Simon our farm dog is sitting in my father's battered armchair. Behind me my mother is riddling the black iron coal-fired range, which cooks our food, heats our water via big copper pipes which rise up to the ceiling, and is the only source of warmth in the house until a fire is lit in the sitting room in the afternoons. In winter we children are allowed to get dressed in front of the range before breakfast, warming ourselves by the open fire door. Up under the ceiling hangs a long wooden clothes-horse, which lowers on cords for wet washing to be spread out for drying, then gets hauled up close to the hot pipes, out of the way. The farmhouse kitchen is the nerve centre of the household. We eat most meals there, dished up straight from the stove onto the old scrubbed pine table: business is done through the open back window with traders and the men, and we listen to the wireless on the dresser.

It is actually a fairly big house, with two front rooms, and an extension to the house called the Big Room. This boasts a huge mahogany fireplace with the mantelpiece supported by two fierce carved giants called Gog and Magog. Upstairs are five bedrooms; behind the kitchen is a scullery with a big sink for rinsing milk churns, and a large old baking oven, no longer in use. Off the Big Room corridor you step down a level to an earth floor: this is the pantry, north facing and always cool, where our milk stands in wide pans for the thick cream to rise. My mother skims it off carefully, and we all have to take a turn winding the paddles of the churn to make it into golden-yellow butter. Cold joints of cooked meat are kept in a grilled safe. The shelves are lined with jars of home-made jams from the fruits of the garden and hedgerows; on the floor are big earthenware crocks full of salted runner and broad beans, and beetroot pickled in vinegar, saved from summer's abundance for winter meals. Bottles of rosehip syrup and elderberry cordial stand ready to cheer the winter's chills.

Outside the scullery door, which is the back door of the house, several paths diverge. One runs up the back garden beside a long hedge, to a gate into the home-field, and on to the cowshed and the poultry houses. Another crosses the side lawn to two pantile roofed coalsheds. These are barely visible beneath the branches of a huge yew tree, which reaches almost to the house. It is said to be about four hundred years old, and is covered in summer with little pink berries, which we mustn't eat because they are poisonous. A third path goes down through an opening in the brick garden wall, past the currant bushes and a large prickly loganberry vine, and out to the farmyard. Our oast house dominates the yard. Unlike most Kentish oasts, which are square with a pyramid on top, our Sussex oast has a circular base with an elegant cone rising to the white painted cowl. However, hops are no longer grown around here, and the oast house serves other purposes now. But the friendly oast, with the cowl which creaks as it turns in the wind, keeps watch over my childhood like our own church spire.

This is where I learn to walk, and run, and play; and where I gradually grow up to young manhood. This is my home.

Remembering

Before me is a grey door. It opens, and I pass through it into a grey room. Against the wall on the right there is a bed under a window: through net curtains a soft yellow sunlight falls on an elderly lady wearing a cotton cap. I move below her face: she looks at me. Then I move away again. It is quite silent; there are no words. When my mother was elderly herself I asked her about this fragment of memory: was it perhaps of the nursing home where I was born, in Heathfield? No, she said, but she recognised the scene: I was about seven months old when she showed me proudly to a family friend in Robertsbridge.

Now it is a sunny spring morning, and I am sitting with my legs tucked under me on the front lawn. Lily the maid has taught me how to press my sharp thumbnails through the stems of daisies, and thread them together: I am making Mummy a daisy chain. But I can't take it to her now. The district nurse came on her bike after breakfast, because Mummy is having a baby. I wonder about time, and how long it takes to have a baby. I can remember last winter, going for walks in the snow. Before that it was sunny and warm, and I could play outside in the garden. And before that I think it was also rainy and cold. But before that, I can't remember anything. Why are there no memories? It's just like the night - you can't see anything. Wasn't I here? Lily comes across the lawn; she is smiling happily and takes my hand. "You can come and see Mummy now" she says, "and you have a baby sister." Mummy is still in bed, although it is the middle of the morning, and she looks covered in perspiration. I give her the daisy chain, but it is too small for a necklace so she puts it on her wrist. Rosemary is a scarlet face surrounded by shawls, lying in the cot. "Isn't she 'dicleous?'" I am told that I said. I was two and a half years old. She was born on the fourteenth of May 1940. My father once said, "she was born on the day that Amsterdam fell, and there has been little peace in Europe since!" (It was a long time before he was forgiven for that one.)

The Shelter

My father and two of the men are digging a hole on the far side of the back lawn. It is quite a deep hole in the vegetable garden, below the apple trees and the summer-house, which always smells heavily of pine and tickles your nose. They are all stripped to the waist and sweating. Later they put curved sheets of metal over the hole, and cover it with earth. There is a low zig-zag stairway to get in. Next day I hear the wail of the siren from Heathfield, going up and down for a long time. We all go down into the shelter. I am sitting on the knee of the paraffin lorry driver, who was delivering fuel when the air-raid warning went. He is reading me a story from my picture book about dragons. Suddenly he says to my father "I'd better move the lorry, it's right outside the house". And he goes out of the shelter to drive it away. It is painted bright red - an obvious target.

On another hot sunny morning a few days later the siren goes again, and we all go down into the shelter. A small oil lamp hangs from the roof - the sort I have in my bedroom at night, as I am not brave about the dark. But it is difficult to read my book by the dim light. There is a strange noise filtering from outside, wailing sounds of engines rising and falling in the air like the noise of midges or gnats, only slower and much louder. My father looks outside and up at the sky. "Come and see this" he says to my mother: one by one we all come up the steps and look upwards. Maybe a dozen little silver crosses are weaving patterns against the blue sky, circling around each other, diving and rising again. There is a distant thumping and banging noise too. One of the crosses suddenly straightens out and flies away, trailing smoke. This is how a dog-fight looks, from the ground. The Battle of Britain is beginning, right over our heads.

The Long Hot Summer

I am making great progress at my picture. First I had coloured Mummy's limed oak bed, and now I am working on the mirror. Mummy comes in, and looks shocked. "Robin, whatever are you doing?" I look back proudly at several feet of bold strokes of scarlet lipstick: "I'se 'witing grass" Whatever Mummy was going to say got lost in the wail of the siren: it happens all the time now. We only go down to the shelter when we hear bombs. So we look out of the window to see the excitement. There is an unusual noise, like an insistent rasping buzzing sound to the engines. Then we see the planes, several of them, flying level and low across the woods from the direction of Brighton. They seem to be quite calm, and not dropping anything. Mummy says "They have to be our boys", and we are leaning out of the bedroom window waving to them. Now they are flying across Selwyns Wood, looking strangely thin, like sticks, painted grey and green. Suddenly my mother stops waving, and stares horrified at the black crosses outlined in white on the fuselages. "Quick - get down - get away from the window - those are Germans!" They are Dornier 17s, the Flying Pencils. I can still hear the sound of those engines in my mind to this day.

Every evening at tea time, my parents listen to the news on the wireless. The announcer tells how many German planes were shot down, and how many of our planes were lost too. Mostly we lost fewer than the Germans. Then comes a day at the end of the summer, when the fighting just didn't stop. The news says that each side lost over a hundred and fifty planes. My Daddy looks very worried. "We cannot go on like this" he says. But the next days are quiet. It seems Goering thought the same.

Winter Christening

It is a cold grey day, and it is a long walk, down and up Browns Lane, across Back Lane, and down again towards Heathfield, then up Newpond Hill, until we turn left through a big farmyard, then up through a wood. All the leaves have fallen, and lie wet on the ground. I am allowed to hold on to the pram, but I can't ride as Rosemary is in it. My feet are cold in my gumboots. Finally we arrive at a small church with a high spire, buried deep in the woods. And this is where Rosemary is christened, at Cross-in-Hand church. I didn't understand what happened. Auntie Yoe and Uncle Tommy are there, and come home with us for tea at the farm afterwards. Grandpa is there too, a cheerful lean man with wiry ginger hair. I only have one Grandpa, who has a farm in Robertsbridge. Yoe and Tommy are my mother's sister and brother. There is another lady too, who is very friendly but difficult to understand: Aunt Cath is my godmother, and she grew up in Belfast.

After tea, when they have all gone away, I go upstairs to bed. At the bend in the stairs is a window which looks north towards the fir grove on our top field. There is a strange red glow all along the sky, although the sun has long since set. "London is burning" Mummy says; "the Germans are dropping bombs on it". It was one of the worst nights of the Blitz. I know London is the biggest city in the world. But I only know a few villages and little towns. London must be very big if the fire goes all along the sky. And what about the poor people? By now the windows have to be covered with blackout curtains. These are made of thick tarred paper on wooden frames, which fit tightly. If a chink of light shows out you will be in trouble with the air-raid wardens, because the Germans may see it and bomb you. I decide that the Germans are very bad indeed.

Further proof of that arrives in a few days. My gas mask has googley eyes and ears that look like Mickey Mouse. In the middle, in front of my nose, is a double flap of rubber, like a duck's beak, which makes a rude noise if you blow out hard. It looks like fun, but it smells of rubber and wheezes when you breathe. I don't like it. Rosemary is too small to wear a gas mask. She has a respirator, like a large khaki coloured egg with a bed inside and windows in the top. She hates it immediately. "Why do we need gas masks anyway?" I ask. "Because in the last war the Germans used poison gas and killed lots of our soldiers", I am told.

Christmas comes and goes. The Big Room becomes a nursery, we live there and sleep there. We have a Christmas tree with some decorations, and I have some toys. The best one is a clockwork car, which one of my uncles had long ago. It is German made. "The Germans made the best toys" someone says. Shortly after that I get a cough. It is not an ordinary cough: it tickles, then turns into a spasm of coughing which turns into a sort of crowing noise. You cough out all your breath, but you can't get any air back. It is horrid. Then Rosemary gets it too. Mummy cradles her in her arms and over her shoulder, patting her desperately as she struggles for air. Whooping cough goes on for six or seven weeks. There is no treatment for it, and everyone is weak from lack of sleep.

1941

The Fir Grove

Wider Horizons

On nice days my mother takes us up for a picnic in D field, at the top of the farm. The farm was named The Old Farm by Grandpa Brown. Mother doesn't like the name, as the farm used to be called Fir Grove Farm, after the cluster of about a dozen old Scots Pines which grow there. A little across from the fir trees there is a cold spring of fresh water, which is captured in a wooden barrel set into the ground, which feeds into a big metal storage tank for the cattle. The bungalow in the corner of the next field is called Little Firs, and was my parents first home when they were married. In fact it was my first home too. They would have preferred to stay there, but Grandpa Brown was a wilful man, and made them move to the farm. I never knew him.

Rosemary is walking now. We play peep-bo around one of the pine trees, and then sit down for tea. The view from our top field just goes on for ever. Over to the east is the ridge behind Heathfield, and the strange shape of the Gibraltar Tower. Further into the distance across the Weald you can see the white cone of the Sugar Loaf - built by a clipper ship captain beside his home, so that he could see it from the Channel. Yet further away is Brightling Beacon, a thin stone needle, where they will light a fire if the invasion happens. Further south, behind the thick oak woods, the country sinks down into the Vale of Sussex, among the most fertile fields in England. Across the eastern horizon stretches the pale blue of the Channel and the whole fifteen miles of Pevensey Bay, from Hastings to Eastbourne. Almost every invasion in English history has happened in Pevensey Bay. From Eastbourne the long bare whalebacks of the Downs stretch all across the southern horizon, from High-and-Over along past Birling Gap and Cuckmere Haven; then Firle Beacon, with Lewes hiding behind it. Then westwards over Possingworth Park you can still see Ditchling Beacon and the dramatic trench of The Devil's Dyke behind Brighton; and on very clear days the view ends at the enigmatic distant hilltop wood called Chanctonbury Ring. Mummy tells us that the Ancient Britons lived at all these places, and used the bare Downs as roadways when the Vale and the Weald were all covered in dense woods. The Downs are not high hills, only six or seven hundred feet tall. As the sun rises on them in the morning you see long shadows outlining folds and valleys, then at midday they mostly go a uniform blue green colour. As the sun sinks westwards a completely different outline slowly becomes clear, as the shadows lengthen and go a dusty purple with the sunset. The Downs are the horizon of my youth.

When the picnic is packed away in its basket, I start running down the field towards home. Rosemary comes toddling behind. I run faster and faster downhill; suddenly there is a big tussock of rough grass in front of me. I try to jump over it, but it trips me and I fall heavily. I try to get up, but I can't breathe, and my legs both hurt badly. Daddy carries me home in his arms. The doctor says that I have sprained both my ankles, and I have to stay in bed for a week.

When finally I can come downstairs again, Grandpa Bonfield has brought a present to cheer me up. Jane is a young Springer Spaniel, with a coat of golden-toast and white, and I adore her. And she adores everybody, and becomes a firm favourite. She is the first dog I have really known on the farm. Though somewhere in the back of my mind I think there was another one - a very big one - but it isn't here any more.

We did not have Jane very long. I am hiding under the kitchen table, crying my eyes out. Grandpa explains that she ran out in front of Coral's big Foden coal lorry, and she was killed. I hate that lorry for ever. He says he will get me another puppy: but I don't want another dog; I want my Jane. And I think my heart will break.

My Sister

I am playing boats in the ditch, which runs from the fir grove down along the bottom of A field, and out to the road. (If we had known what was in that ditch, everyone would have been horrified.) Rosemary wants to play too, but our mother insists it is time to go home to bed. "Why do I always have to go to bed first? Why not Robin?" "Because he's older; he was born first." "Well, when will I be born first?!"

We are standing with Mummy in B and R.Q Clarkson's Post Office, Stationers, and General Stores. It is a muddy and wet autumn, and the lady at the counter has splashed mud all up her stockings and skirt. Rosemary giggles: "Look Mummy, messy lady". This is ignored. So it is repeated. "Yes. Shh dear." "But she *is* a messy lady!" insists Rosemary, very loudly, to glares from everyone present.

The Flying Standard

It is nearly Christmas again, and Daddy takes me to look at the toyshops in Heathfield on the way home from market. But they are almost empty, just bare shelves, with one beautiful bear in the front window. Mrs Murphy says "It's the war: there is nothing left to sell now. I don't know what we'll do."

We have a big car, a blue-black one with a big Union Jack on the radiator. It doesn't often get used, as petrol is in short supply. But the farm has a small petrol ration, to take the day-old chicks to the market. Dad is very proud of the car, which has a very big engine. They call it The Flying Standard sometimes. The engine has a deep throbbing note, as we pull away down Heathfield High Street. I am kneeling on the back seat, looking through the rear window and I watch that lovely bear until it fades from sight. On Christmas morning, beside my stocking, is a familiar shape. I unwrap it quickly - Rupert!

1942

Soldiers

Rosemary is getting pretty mobile now. We both had new gumboots for Christmas: mine are red and hers are white. It takes forever to go for walks in the snow, she is so proud of her boots, she keeps stopping to brush the snow off them.

Spring comes again. There are changes around the farm now. Soldiers are everywhere. They are mostly Canadians, and they live in the camp which has appeared in Possingworth Park, across Warren Lane, behind our Woodfield. Possingworth Park is a lovely place, with huge redwood cedar trees and a big lake, half as big as our farm. It should really be private, but the big house has become an hotel, and sometimes Mummy takes us swimming or paddling in the shallow part of the lake, between the islands and the shore. The camp is right opposite Woodfield. The soldiers live in strange huts, made of big circular sections of corrugated iron.

Lily the maid has gone. I don't know where. She was nice, and I miss her. Now we have Dorry, but she is not much help. She takes Rosemary for walks sometimes. Rosemary asks Mummy "Do I have to go for walks with Dorry?" "Why, what's wrong with the walks?" "Well we never go anywhere. We just stand outside the camp, and I get so cold while she talks to the soldiers." Dorry didn't last long.

The camp doctor is living with us at the farm; his name is Doctor Bell, and he and Mrs Bell have moved into the Big Room. Mummy says they are 'billeted', and she cooks meals for them. One morning she comes back with the breakfast tray, absolutely shocked. "They poured maple syrup all over their bacon!", she says. "Maybe that's what Canadians do?" my father wonders.

The soldiers are from Quebec; and they are in England to help us win the war. Every morning they are on the road outside the farm, stripped to the waist, doing rifle drill and exercises under the eye of their drill sergeant, in a mixture of English and some other language. One morning I think I will have some fun. I creep along behind the garden wall. The whole company can see me, all except for the drill sergeant. I pop up from my shelter, draw a bead on his sweating back with my water pistol, and squeeze the trigger. There is a roar of laughter from the troops, and a rather different roar from the sergeant. I don't understand all the details of what he says - but I don't think he is pleased!

There are a lot of words that I don't understand. My Daddy slices chunks of hay out of the haystack, to feed the animals. The hay-knife is a wicked thing, bigger than me, with a broad handle across the top for two hands. As the season goes on the haystack gets ever smaller, until it is just like a loaf standing on end, about eight feet square and six feet tall. Daddy is on the top, slicing downwards, when the whole pile totters and falls over. He lands, buried up to the waist in hay. Fortunately the hay-knife, which could have cut him in half, fell the other side. He says a long word, very loudly. I go back to the kitchen window, and tell Mummy what happened, and ask what the word means. She laughs out loud. But she does not explain.

A few days later two soldiers are walking up the road, and start looking up at the house and shouting. I run to tell Mummy - "The soldiers say to get in the honey!" She looks puzzled for a moment, then flies upstairs, and comes down with an indignant Rosemary in her arms. She was balanced on my parents bedroom window-sill, playing above a twelve foot drop onto the rockery. The soldier explains - "I said for God's sake get in, honey!" Saving England begins with saving my little sister.

Robertsbridge

Sometimes I go to stay for a few days at Robertsbridge, at Grandpa's house at the bottom of the village High Street. It is the farmhouse for his farm, and Uncle Tommy runs a garage next door - C & A Bonfield, Automobile Engineers. Except that during the war there are few cars on the roads, and he has turned it into a small factory making parts for aeroplanes. He says the government's idea is that the Germans can bomb big factories, but they can never find hundreds of little ones. He has about six lathes in the garage, and the spirals of aluminium that come off the metal fascinate me. All the turnings are carefully swept up from the floor, as aluminium is very precious. It is used to build Spitfires, which are still fighting above our heads quite often. My mother gave all our aluminium saucepans to a collection, so the Spitfires can have longer wings and fly higher than the Germans.

My mother told me about Grandpa's farms. "When I was a young girl, we used to live at Whitwell in Hertfordshire. Grandpa rented a farm on the estates of the Bowes Lyon family; and Queen Elizabeth is their daughter. Your Godmother, Alla Knight, is a sister of Grannie Bonfield, and was the Queen's nursery nurse. But Grandpa always wanted to own his own farm. So one day he hired a whole train, and moved all his stock and all the farm equipment to Etchingham, together with all our family, and we had a farm there. But a year later there was a very bad drought, and a lot of farms failed, and soon we moved to Brightling Hall. It was a big impressive place to live, but Yoe and I knew it was haunted. Footsteps ran upstairs, but there was never anyone there. Grannie said that once someone came downstairs, the kitchen door opened; no-one came in, but the dogs looked up, and their eyes followed something across the room. Then the back door swung open, and swung shut again. I didn't like it there. So I was happy when we moved to Robertsbridge." Another time she told us stories of Whitwell. "Your grandfather was naughty when he was a little boy. He went swimming in the lake in the big park with the village boys. The keeper heard them; first he collected up all their clothes. Then he set up a hue and cry, and chased them back through the streets to their homes, naked as jay-birds! Their parents had to go to him and plead for their son's clothes back". "And then there was the village drunk at Harpendon. One night he went rolling through the village shouting "Two moons tonight! Two moons tonight!" All the windows opened, and all the old ladies looked out: "Where, where Mr Sands?" "One up in the sky; one down in the River Lea. Two moons tonight!"

Robertsbridge

Grandpa loves all animals. He used to have a **favourite** horse called Major, who had once been an army horse in an artillery regiment. Whenever Major heard a brass band, (there used to be lots in those days), he would gallop the length of the farm to get near, and march up the hedgerows beside the band with his tail held high. Grandpa still has a sheepdog, a little **black** and white Welsh Collie called Psyche. She is clever and obedient, but mortally afraid of guns and thunder. One afternoon after lunch, Grandpa is sitting in his chair in the kitchen, beside the big white Esse range, quietly reading. A thunder-storm is rumbling about somewhere, and Psyche gets more and more fidgety. Suddenly a flash of lightning and a huge crack of thunder go off together, almost overhead. Poor Psyche springs from the rug - straight through Grandpa's Daily Express - and lies there trembling in his lap while he still holds the two halves of his shattered paper!

There is another reason I like Robertsbridge - they have oast houses here too. And here, closer to Kent, they are still working at their proper job - which is drying hops. The hops grow in fields which are covered in long lines of poles eight foot high, and linked with wires and strings. When the hop harvest comes round at the end of August, all the East End of London

Hops

takes a working holiday. The Kent Cockneys come down by train, and camp in any rooms or even sheds they can find, or in tents that the farmers put up for them. The whole family sets-to, pulling the hop vines down, and stripping the leafy cones of the hops into big sacks for the oast houses. Once dried, the brewers buy the hops to flavour their beer. Kentish hops are famous, and this part of the country is called 'The Garden of England'.

Dad, the AFS, and the Windmill

Farmers don't get called up, as Britain needs to eat if it is going to win the war. But even farmers have war duties to do. Once a week Dad goes up to the windmill at Cross-in-Hand, which is the best viewpoint for miles. He spends the nights watching for fires or bombing raids. They have a small lorry with a water tank and a trailor-pump, and form a three man fire brigade. It is called the Auxiliary Fire Service. Because they are watching, their job is to try to get to fires while they are still small, and to contain the damage until the big Fire Engines can get to the scene.

One morning I come downstairs, and find the front door locked. It has never been locked in all my life. My mother explains to Dad at breakfast. "About three in the morning I heard voices. Two soldiers were sitting on our garden wall, smoking. One said to the other "I think she's alone, yer know"; and he said "D'yer fancy yer luck?" So I crept downstairs, and turned the key. It went with a big clunk. I heard one say "There mate, she's locked yer' out!"

The windmill is at the top of Dads Hill, just behind Cross-in-Hand. It is a big post mill, with a low circular building at the base, and a sort of house with an arched roof above it which turns with the wind: the sails are on an axle which goes through the building just below the roof. It is kept facing the wind by a smaller windmill - called a fan tail - that runs on a circular track around the hilltop, and which pushes the mill around on a strong beam like a boat's tiller. The sails come down almost to the ground when it is turning, and then go sweeping high up into the sky, making a sort of rushing noise like a distant waterfall. Once Rosemary and I are allowed to explore the mill while it is going. Everything, even the gearwheels on the big shaft in the roof, is made of plain white wood, dusty with flour. The sacks of corn are hauled up to the top floor on a chain through double trap-doors in each floor; they open upwards for the sacks, and then drop back shut so you can't fall through. The corn goes into big hoppers, and then it falls through slides, which are vibrating all the time, into a hole in the top of a pair of big millstones, which are turning slowly. The flour and the husks of the corn fall out the sides of the millstones onto sieves, which are shaken to carry the husks away for bran. Then the flour falls down a chute to a lower floor, where it goes through another pair of millstones. Finally on the ground floor the flour falls down a chute into sacks, for the bakers or the farmers to use. While it is working and the sails are swooshing around, the whole windmill throbs in every plank; it is like being inside a living animal. There is another mill building, for when there is no wind. This is driven by a coal-gas engine with an enormous flywheel, which goes up to the first story windows. On still days you can hear its slow musical chonk-chonk-chonk all through the village. Jack Newnham, the miller, is one of my father's best friends.

1943

School

New Year arrives, with a sullen roar of planes overhead. A small formation of three bombers flies directly over the farm: they are ours - I can see the red white and blue roundels. Just like the song "There'll always be er Ningland", sung by a stentorian sergeant major voice, which is always on the wireless. We truly believe so, though it would be nice if the war was over, I think privately. "Red white and blue, what does it mean to you?" - it means you don't have to sit under the table, or go out to the shelter. But things are changing for me too.

On the first day my father took me by bus to Murrays School, in Horam. I think I was the only one who started for the spring term. I already know my alphabet as a song my mother taught me. But I learned to repeat the LMNOP section to fit with the song, and the school floors me because they go straight on with QRST. Of course they are wrong, but I thought better of pointing this out! Anyway, the lunch is quite good. After school Anne and Nicholas Pearcy collect me , and we all go home on the bus which stops at the farm gate. Ding! " Ol' Farm" calls the conductor. "And what did you have for lunch?", asks Mummy. "Pink remange with jam on top!" School isn't too bad.

Nicholas becomes my best friend. He is slightly younger than me; he has lots of Meccano and we both love machines, so he is fascinated with the farm. We have a noisy Lister engine to drive our machines, like the food mixer and the dynamo. The dynamo charges a roomful of batteries in glass tanks, which fizzle and make choking smells. These run the fans in the incubators. If the fans stop any time in the three weeks it takes to hatch eggs, then the chicks may die; and my father does not trust the mains electricity supply. There are big switches, like knife blades, which make fat blue sparks when they are opened. We play with these for a long time, until we find something else to do. The dynamo discharged the batteries for hours, until my father found it running like a motor. This was serious. But I don't think I got worse than a warning about it.

Murrays school is less easy to please. We are learning to play cricket, under-arm bowling and big-swipe batting. I am fielding, and a lucky hit takes a ball past me out of reach. "Damn" I say, just like a grown-up. Two young girls are shocked:

"Oo umm, I'ner tell!" And they run away. Shortly after that I am called in to Mr Murray's study. "You said a rude word. What was it?" "I don't remember". So I had one whack with a slipper to help me remember what I must not say. My father hears the story with concern, but not for me. "Does this often happen?" he asks. "What, the spankings?" "No, the 'telling' on people?" I say the children at Murrays are supposed to 'report' on others, though I never have. Father says "I won't have my son taught to be an informer. This sounds like socialism!" It is almost the end of the school term, and I don't go back to Murrays. This is a great relief for another reason, as I will not have to see Horam Manor. This huge building opposite the bus stop has been hit by an incendiary bomb. Above a line of tall laurels you can see the blackened beams of the roof: it fills me with horror to see their charred arms reaching up helplessly to the sky. I have never seen a bad fire, but just the sight of burnt ruins strikes something completely elemental in me. I cannot bear to look at it.

Anne Pearcy is eight, quite big and responsible. She and Nicholas have two older half-sisters, Heather and Diana. I ask Nicholas how you get half-sisters? He explains that they all have the same mother, but she married his father after she already had the first two girls. He did not know their father, they never speak about him. He is in mortal fear of his own father though. His father has some connection with the Navy: he has a black beard, neatly trimmed, and is very stern. They all live in a big white house called 'Instanter', and Mr Pearcy's law is unbending. He has his own yacht, but no-one is allowed to use yachts during the war. Except with the famous 'Little Ships' at Dunkirk. He says "I was just loading up with our boys, when a Messerschmitt strafed the yacht. I thought we would all be killed. But the bullets went through the compass, and the alcohol splashed my face. I licked my lips, and felt a lot better! And we got back to Shoreham."

When I asked my parents what happened to Diana and Heather's father, they paused. "We hear him sometimes on the wireless. He comes on after the BBC stops at night, on a programme called 'Germany Calling'. "Why does he do that?", I ask. "He works for the Germans now. His name is William Joyce, but everyone calls him Lord Haw-Haw, because of the nasty way he laughs about news he gets of England." "What does he say?" "He talks about things around here. He says the troops must not wear their boots when they dance at the State Hall in Heathfield, as it will spoil the floor. He says when Germany wins the war, Hitler will make him the Gauleiter of Sussex. He is a traitor." I think a Gauleiter is probably bad. But anyway, he is not Nicholas's father, and he is gone now. We still play any time we can. But Nicholas is often kept in. They don't trust him, as he runs away from home sometimes. Once he walked almost to Uckfield, which is six miles away. Sometimes, when I am cross, I say "I'll run away down Warren Lane". But nobody believes me. Warren Lane is only at the back of the farm beyond Woodfield; and I have never done it anyway.

Sherry and Simon

My mother wants to have a farm dog, or preferably several. So a very doggy sort of lady, Miss Sylvia Nairn, arrives from London with a tubby dark golden puppy. This is Sherry, who is a little golden retriever bitch. She has a very expensive pedigree, it seems. As she grows bigger, she becomes a devoted guard dog for us children, and keeps a watchful eye on anyone coming to the farm. She is not above nipping the ankles of anyone she does not trust. A few months later Auntie Sylvia brings a very dirty little jelly roll of a puppy, so nervous that he hid under the seat from the ticket collector on the train. " 'Ere, wot you tryin' to 'ide under there?" A very sooty Simon was produced, and Southern Railways solemnly punched his ticket. As soon as he enters the house, Sherry seizes him and throws him back down the front steps, to put him in his place in the household! Simon is also a pedigree golden retriever, but he never makes it as a showdog. He is a throwback to the original race, which came from Siberia. He is half as big again as a show dog, and probably twice as heavy. His coat is not golden, but shaggy sandy-white; and his bark can be heard in Waldron, nearly two miles away. And he wouldn't harm a fly, being too trusting and good natured by half - then.

Sherry however is a total snob. She hates the dustmen when they come to empty the dustbins - all except for one, whom she almost ushers into the garden. He has a cultivated Oxford accent!

Simon and Robin

The Italians

The farm workers have all gone now, joined up as soldiers or sailors. Dave Fenner, one of the most trusted men, was at Singapore when it fell to the Japanese, and no-one even knows if he is still alive. Now we have extra help from Land Girls in the Land Army, who wear khaki jodhpurs and dark green jumpers. They are cheerful women who come to do any jobs on the farm; if they don't know how to do something, my father teaches them. They say it's better than working in a factory anyway.

Then there are the Italians. They are Prisoners of War, who live in a camp miles away, near Warbleton. They come to the farm in a big maroon bus every morning, and my mother cooks them lunch. They don't need guards, as nobody wants to escape. Nobody ever escaped from England anyway: there are no boats, and it is too far to swim. In any case they say they are happy here. My mother says one lunchtime "That has never happened before. The carpenter sat on the roof of one of the chicken houses, and sang me serenades from the opera! And they all joined in, in harmony."

The Italians miss their own children though. One of them made a beautiful ring out of glass, and set three little coloured fragments in it like jewels, as a present for Rosemary. But when he went to lift her onto his knee, to try on the ring, Sherry took his wrist in her jaw to stop him. She didn't bite, but just made it clear that liberties with her children were not permitted.

One summer afternoon I am listening to the wireless by myself - I have learned how to turn it on and find the different stations - when I hear something important. I run round the house to find my father: "Daddy, Daddy, the wireless says that Italy has just surrendered!" To my surprise he seems unimpressed: "Oh" he says, "I thought they probably would". But it is not the end of the war - far from it. Soon the Italians go home by ship to Italy, and there are no more arias in the fields.

The wireless tells of other strange people too. There is Devil Eire, who is the bad chief of Eire, which is what they call Ireland now. It used to be part of Britain, but their government hates the English so much that they will not fight the Germans, and hope that if the Germans punish England they will not invade Ireland. "They are traitors, and they are fools too" says my father. "If England falls, they will not last a week". Even so, it seems that a lot of the Irish people have joined the British army, as they do not believe their own government. The world is a complicated place.

Developments

My father cannot believe his eyes. Grandpa Bonfield has chosen him a cow, which arrives in a lorry. Daisy walks cautiously down the ramp, and just goes on and on. Dad sags back against the garage in disbelief: she must be the biggest Guernsey cow ever born. But she is a gentle creature, content and endlessly patient; her steamy breath smells of fresh milk, which she provides for us for the next fourteen years. Daisy is soon a part of the family. Not long afterwards she is joined by Bluebell, a black and white Freisian, almost as big as Daisy. Grandpa could certainly pick them. The milking herd is launched. In future years we have a dozen milking cows, and with the steers and heifers the herd runs close to twenty. Dad works our twenty six acres pretty hard.

The petrol ration gets smaller. Dad decides to have a pony and trap, and Jezebel arrives at the farm. No horse was ever better named, near-black in looks and heart. Jezebel is sullen and lazy, with a calculating mean streak. If anyone approaches with harness in hand she looks sideways at them and lays her ears back. Then she shifts casually, and steps heavily on their feet. Dad only gets her between the shafts a few times. She drags the trap a hundred yards along Browns Lane, to the beginning of the downhill slope. Knowing that downhill means returning uphill, she balks. When he finally wheels her round, she sets off at a canter, and is back at the farm in seconds. One other time he got her down the road to Rosers Cross, at the junction with Warren Lane. There used to be a blacksmiths shop there, and Jezebel went to be shod - she hated it. But smiths can deal with recalcitrant horses, and for once she did not get her own way. She flew back to the farm, with Dad hanging on to the trap for dear life. Hopes for becoming a country gentleman this way are abandoned, and Jezebel is left to her own devices with the cows. It may be that they didn't like her either. One day she is found, drowning in the D-Field spring. She has her fore legs sunk deep into the mud below the barrel. It worked like quicksand - her struggles only made them sink deeper. The combined strength of Dad and everyone else were incapable of lifting her out. She was not a good horse, but she deserved a better end than that. Mother thinks that the cows jostled her in.

I am fascinated with the forge. The dark smoky shed is open in all weathers. In the forge there is a charcoal fire on an open hearth; and huge bellows, six feet long and a yard wide, hang from the roof and blow the fire to white heat, so it is painful to look at it. The smith in his leather apron picks up horseshoes with long tongs, puts them in the fire till they are glowing orange, and he beats them with a hammer over a big anvil with a devil's horn on the side. Then he plunges the shaped iron into a barrel of water, and the steam hisses and fills the shed with a choking metallic smell and taste. Sometimes in the deepest parts of the woods we come upon the charcoal burners camps, with their wooden piles buried under turfs, smouldering slowly. The people there are silent, and somehow a race apart. Their skin and clothes are filthy dirty, and if you say hello they never reply. Some people say they are gypsies, but no-one seems to know.

Rosemary and I go to stay with Granny Brown. She lives in Croydon, in a smart town house in Blenheim Crescent. She is a rather frail and bent elderly lady, and she has lovely things in her house. There are beautiful nymphs and shepherdesses made of translucent Delph Porcelain, and ivory chess sets from China, and two beautiful grandfather clocks whose soft chimes drift through the house. But best of all, she is a wonderful pastry cook, and she loves cooking for appreciative children! Then in the afternoon sometimes she plays the piano for us. She has a huge piano with a German name, and she plays so intently that she seems to forget we are there. When she gets to the end, she just looks into space for a little while: then she sighs, and says "Would you like some more cake?". When we get back home, we learn that we have a new sister. That is a surprise, as we had not realised that she was on the way. Penelope she is named, and this is promptly shortened to Penny. She is long and thin, and for months she wouldn't put on weight. Mummy is very worried, and is up half the nights nursing her. Eventually she starts growing properly, and the family relaxes a bit.

One day I am walking beside the pram, going with Mummy up to the village. As we get towards the bottom of the dip by French's farm, a solitary German fighter comes streaking across from the west. A Spitfire is following closely. Mummy scoops up the girls, and we get down in the ditch beside the road. There is a rattle of heavy machine guns, and the ack-ack from the woods on Beacon Hill beside the windmill joins in the firing. The German plane starts smoking, turns upside down, and something falls out. Then a parachute suddenly blossoms like a dirty mushroom, right over us. The plane goes into a nosedive, the engine note goes up steadily to a scream, and it crashes into the woods over towards Little London. A column of black smoke spurts upwards towards the sky, and a few seconds later a rolling boom echoes across to us. The parachute comes down two fields away. The pilot does not even fall over, he just gathers in the lines. Two of the Frenches are running down the field to capture him: one is carrying a pitchfork.

Tavistock Hall

I have a new school for the autumn term. It is closer than Murrays, as it is in Heathfield, little more than two miles away. And it is a rather tougher sort of place. But soon after I get there the playground is dug up to make trenches outside the classrooms. Every time the siren goes off we all pour out into the trenches: it sounds like fun, but it isn't when it's raining. We have assembly and roll call, then morning prayers and a hymn before classes start. I suppose that everyone in England knows the hymn tunes from those days. We have all the subjects, not simply the three Rs. I am expected to learn French, my tables up to twelve times twelve, and as soon as that is done we start on multiplication and division. It is not easy. And we have special talks from the Air Raid Wardens. They show us the little bombs that the German planes drop, sometimes called 'Butterfly Bombs', which land harmlessly, but then blow up if you touch them. There are also explosive toys, and we are told never to touch a toy found in surprising places: just tell the wardens. There is also a warning about what looks like silver paper, but is actually lots of aluminium foil which planes are dropping to deceive the radar. Of course at that time radar itself is a secret. We are all told that our RAF pilots can see the enemy planes at night because they eat lots of carrots! We believe it; but the story was planted to get back to the Germans.

One of the things I like about Tavistock is the great woods down the back of the hill behind the school. They go on for miles, and in the course of school exercise and nature walks along the unmade tracks we explore a huge stretch of wild woodland. About a mile down from school you come to the railway line, then on downhill to a deserted sawmill camp, with its abandoned steam engines. After another mile you come down to a lonely lake called Isinghurst Pond, a strange dark brooding place which is back downhill from

Hawthorn Flowers

Cross-in-Hand. From there the woods run on for miles to Five Ashes, but we seldom go much further, as we are already a long way from the school.

The railway is a single track line called 'The Cuckoo Line'. Legend and tradition have it that 'The Old Woman of Heathfield lets the first cuckoo out of her basket at Heffle Fair for the start of lawful spring in England'. (Heffle is Sussex dialect for Heathfield). Heffle Fair used to be on the 15th of April; but they don't have it now because of the war. Anyway, the gradient up from Mayfield is quite steep, and we watch the steam locomotives labouring slowly up the hill, until the train plunges into the short tunnel right under Heathfield High Street, to emerge with a rush and a whistle just beside the station platform.

All country children need the lessons of nature walks for their own Foxglove safety. A surprising number of the flowers and berries to be found in the banks and hedgerows are harmful, and some are outright poisonous. Woody Nightshade, or Bryony, will give you stomach ache: but the black fruit of the dark blue and yellow Deadly Nightshade, also called Belladonna, can kill you. The elegant red candles of Lords and Ladies will do you no good, and you should wash your hands after picking the lovely Foxgloves, which can make your heart race out of control. Cow parsley is harmless, but the rather similar Hemlock is deadly. Rose hips and blackthorn haws are useful, and we pick them in summer for the chemists to collect for making into Rosehip Syrup, which we have for vitamin C in winter. Elderberries are edible, but Wayfarer and Yew berries are not. Damsons and sloes and crab apples are all edible when cooked carefully, but don't try them from the hedges when raw. Of course, blackberries in August make delicious jam, and wild strawberries in June and July are nature's healthy sweets for children. Never eat mushrooms, they might be toadstools: your parents will probably show you the differences when you are bigger. But we think that life is more interesting for us than it would be in a town, with only dusty playgrounds to play in.

Hawthorn Haws

1944

The Tide Turns

Christmas comes and goes, and 1944 comes in less with a bang than with a steady growling sound, that fills the whole sky and seems to go on all day. The Air Force is sending ever larger numbers of bombers - thousands - over to bomb Germany now, and the planes form up over Sussex and Kent before flying off to the continent. One day we are out in the car, delivering chickens, and we go past the new airfield at Upper Dicker, near Hailsham. And there, on the other side of the road, with its nose poking through the hedge and all its window glass smashed, is a bomber. I think "How sad. It must have got damaged by ack-ack fire, and made it all the way home, only to fall short by the width of a country lane." It doesn't occur to me that it might be even sadder for the Germans: they started it, and now they are getting what they asked for.

Books are given away at school, showing all the planes of The Allies, as we are called now. Big American planes called Flying Fortresses, bristling with guns, are flying the day bombing raids, and the lighter armed Lancasters and Halifaxes of the RAF are flying at night. The books boast about the bombing. "Remember Plymouth, and Coventry, and the London Blitz? Well, it's Germany's turn now. Every night our planes are hitting the munitions factories of the Ruhr and the Rhineland." A distant cousin of mine on the Bonfield side is a pilot. His family prepared a big surprise party for his twenty-first birthday. But he never knew: he was shot down the night before. He never came back.

Propaganda is everywhere. In the Post Office, in the bus shelters, you see the slogan "Careless talk costs lives" with a picture of two men chatting, and a third suspicious character furtively listening. Then there is The Squanderbug. This ugly thing looks like an enormous green louse, with devil's horns and a nasty long scorpion tail, and it is carelessly throwing money around in shops. In truth, everything is rationed, and there is very little to buy. But Nicholas has a big Squanderbug poster on his bedroom wall. Typically - he is rather fond of it. Mrs Hall, our neighbour up the road at Little Firs, is talking to my father. "The wardens and the police have searched the bungalow three times in the last fortnight. It seems that people in Waldron think I am signalling to the German planes with a flashing mirror. After all, how does Lord Haw-Haw get his news? Finally they found a loose glass in the little diamond-paned windows in the lounge, which shakes in the wind. It seemed to satisfy them, anyway."

There are strange things to be seen in the sky sometimes. The familiar Dakotas fly over with strange boxy looking planes following them. If you look carefully you can see they are joined by a rope: the Dakotas are towing gliders. Nobody knows why you would want to tow planes that seem to have no engines: what are they for? We soon found out.

The farm across the road, between us and Selwyns Wood, belongs to Mr Field. He is a cheerful man, with a red round face and bushy white eyebrows - a bit like a beardless Father Christmas in fact. He takes his milk churns in a wheelbarrow up to the stand for the milk lorry, on the corner of Browns Lane, and he often gives Rosemary and me a ride back in the barrow. My bedroom faces across the road to a gate into his field. One grey and foggy morning I get up and look out of the window, and I cannot believe my eyes. The whole field is full of lorries and tents; and right in front of Mr Field's gate a field gun is pointing straight into my bedroom window. There are soldiers in our farmyard, and in most of the buildings too. A captain tells my father in the foodstore "This is my command post: we are on manoeuvres". My father says "Well, manoeuvres or not, the stock must be fed. You won't mind if I get on with the farm work?" The officer waves dismissively. So Dad starts up the Lister. The radio and the command post vanish in less than a minute to somewhere much quieter! It seems as if the whole of England has become an army camp. There are soldiers everywhere, and long convoys of army lorries fill the roads. Military police stand at every crossroads, as all the signposts were taken down long ago to make it more difficult for invaders, and the convoys cannot find their own way.

The Gun

Then quite suddenly the roads are empty. The tanks on their long trailers have gone, the Bren-Gun carriers are not tearing up the roads with their tracks, and everything is quiet. The camp in Possingworth Park is almost empty: the soldiers have gone. Three days later the BBC announces that the D Day invasion of France has happened. Gliders and paratroops have landed in Normandy at midnight, and the troops landed on the Normandy Beaches at dawn. The rest is history. And Sussex becomes a much quieter place for a few weeks.

Haymaking, Harvests and Picnics.

While the troops are fighting their way slowly across France, the countryside turns back to its summer business. School is over, and the haymaking has already begun. The War Agricultural Board, called the War-Ag by everyone, took over nearly all the agricultural machinery at the beginning of the war, and all the farmers try to book a tractor to help with the work. But when the hay and the crops ripen suddenly, there are not enough tractors or drivers to work for everybody. You can cut hay with a horse-drawn mower, so the remaining farm horses are pressed into action. The cut grass lies in the sun for a couple of days, smelling of English summer. Then the men toss it in the air with pitchforks, so it can dry on both sides. The farmers take turns to help their neighbours with any machines they have. Grandad French comes with his hay rake; the horse trots over the field while the wide rake of semi-circular tines gathers up the hay. Then, with a pull on a lever, the tines lift up in the air and the hay is left gathered into a long line across the field. Then the men and the land-girls pile it up into little haystacks, called stooks, to try to keep it dry. Grandad French is blind in one eye; one day he fell under the hay rake. When the hay is properly dry, the hay wagon pulled by a horse, or tractor, or anything else available, is piled high with the hay; and it is taken back to the farmyard to build the haystack. To make up for the lack of tractors, we have a very old car, a bull-nose Morris Cowley tourer, which pulls the carts over the fields. It is very difficult to start, and often backfires like a gun; the blue sparks in the dynamo are visible under the remains of the dashboard. We call it The Summercar, and it only comes out for harvests.

Our mother makes picnic teas for everyone during haymaking, and takes the sandwiches and drinks out to the side of the field. And there we sit for a few peaceful minutes, with the birds calling in the hedges, and the smell of the pale mauve watermint all around us. The great treat for Rosemary and me is to ride on top of the hay cart back to the farm. New hay is so soft that you can sink into it until you are almost out of sight. And the heady perfume of fresh-dried grasses and clover and all the other flowers of the fields is almost overpowering.

Harvesting the grain starts with a hard job for a man with a scythe. The corn is planted right to the edge of our small Sussex fields. But the binder, which is a mower with flails on, has to be drawn by a tractor. So as not to lose the grain, the first pass around the field has to be cut by hand. Then the binder cuts the rest, and ties the stalks up into sheaves, with the grains of corn still on the stalks. The workers follow behind the binder, gathering six or eight sheaves together and standing them up carefully in stooks to dry. After a few days they are loaded onto a cart and once more piled up into a corn stack - wheat or barley, or oats, the most delicate crop of all. The stacks are shaped like a building, with a pitched roof, so that most of the rain runs off the sides. Then in the autumn the threshing team comes round the farms, to separate the grain from the straw of the stalks.

But we do not see the threshing this year.

Doodlebug Summer

Doodlebug - The Flying Bomb

I am woken up by a very strange sound. It is like a very big motorbike engine, the sort that despatch-riders use, only very fast and very loud. It seems to come from everywhere, and when it fades away again it is impossible to guess where it went. I don't think it was on the road. It is just getting light, still grey on a very early summer morning. That was the second flying bomb to cross the Channel; the first one flew over Dover before dawn. We soon find out what made the strange sound, and this time we can see it. It looks like a small plane, smaller than a fighter, with a tube on supports above the fuselage at the back. This tube is a sort of jet engine, like a pulsed blow-lamp, which is what makes all the noise. It is in fact driven by a rapid series of explosions. And in the front is a very big bomb. This is Hitler's Vergeltungswaffe or Revenge-Weapon, the V1. They fly in the general direction of London either until they run out of fuel, or the engine is switched off and they dive into the ground. We learn that while the motorbike sound is running, you have little to fear. When it stops you had better find shelter, quickly.

I am hiding under the dining-room table: we can hear a doodlebug is coming. Then the noise stops, but no bang follows; and then it starts again. Puzzled, we go out into the road to see what is happening. A doodlebug is flying quite low, aiming just past the farm. The engine is faltering: it must have been damaged by ack-ack over the coast. Mrs Hall is looking down the road at it, and we are looking up the road, so it is very close. As it passes us, the engine stops again; and we dive for the cover of the garden wall, as it is certain to hit our D field hill. I think just as it gets there the engine re-starts for a few seconds, and it clears the hill. A few seconds later there is an enormous explosion when it lands in the tennis courts of Possingworth Park, and blows out all the windows for miles.

Two days later Rosemary and I go on an unexpected journey. Penny is not yet a year old, and a delicate infant at that. She stays at home with our mother. As my father told it years later - "I had to be careful what I wrote, because of the censors. So I sent Eric and Gladys a telegram saying 'Resort conditions deteriorating. Meet children Paddington 11 am tomorrow'." Auntie Gladys is my father's sister. That night we sleep in strange beds in Derbyshire; at Milford, at the south end of the Peak District.

Derbyshire

Bowns Green looks like quite a small house on the outside, a sandstone cottage near the top of the hill east of Milford, looking west over the Derwent valley. It stands a quarter of a mile along its own entrance drive off the hill road, in a garden behind a large and rather wild orchard. But somehow, on the inside, the two-up two-down house is bigger than it looks. There is a modern kitchen built onto the south end. And beneath the steep roof there are two more low rooms, which smell of apples stored over the last winter; stocked with the sort of fascinating jumble that people collect, and then put away and forget. Low windows at floor level look out over the orchard and the garden. Rosemary and I spend happy hours up there, dressing up in old finery and looking at old photo albums. Before long we are taken round to be introduced to the neighbours. Auntie Gladys does not have children of her own, and seems quite pleased to have us for a while. The nearest neighbours, the Watsons, try to survive on a smallholding of less than three acres, with just two cows and a few chickens. In summer they go barefoot, and sometimes in winter too Auntie says. They are often ill, and she helps them with medicines.

A footpath runs down to Milford village, skirting around several fields of recently harvested wheat till it comes to Redfearns Farm. This is a big dairy farm with a large herd and a very mucky farmyard. The farmhouse is a dour dark grey place built of gritstone; it seems so gloomy that the cheerful people who live there come as a surprise. Mr Redfearn is a farmer straight out of a picturebook, wearing a loose smock, a cloth cap, trousers tied with twine above his boots, and always chewing on a straw. He asks us questions about our farm, but his

Derbyshire country accent is rather hard to understand until you get used to it. He tries Rosemary's name over a few times, then decides to call her Posy instead. She was polite about it, but told me after that she hated it. Mrs Redfearn is a jolly soul whose children have grown up and gone: every time we pass by, collecting fresh milk in a little churn, she has freshly baked cakes for us. The gingerbread is especially good.

Gloster Gladiators

From the other side of the farmyard the path crosses a small field, then you come to the top of a very steep stairway made of cut sandstone, which goes straight down the hillside into the middle of Milford. Down one more street and you come out by the River Derwent, which is the biggest river I have ever seen. There is a bridge for the road west to Duffield and Derby; and lower down the river is a weir, a sort of dam with a stone waterslide down to the lower level. Along the road at the end of the village is a big building called The Mill. It used to be a textile mill, driven by the water wheels underneath from the higher level above the weir. But now it is the Genic Chemical Factory, and it belongs to Uncle Eric. The mill has a number of different production lines. One is making the strongly scented cakes of crystals that slowly dissolve in toilet bowls. There are air freshener chemicals as well. But our favourite is the sugar syrup refinery on the ground floor. They start with the raw molasses left over from cane sugar manufacture. Then this is heated with steam, and separated in a number of basins stirred by big steel spoons, until it becomes refiners syrup. This is delicious, thinner and somehow both less sweet and more tasty than Lyles Golden Syrup: it goes to the bakers to make cakes and biscuits. And to us, in big spoonfuls!

I am fascinated by the trains on the LMS railway, which runs across the whole view through Duffield and on up to Belper. There is a tunnel a mile long under Holgrove Hill. Some trains are so long that the engines have come out one side before the guards van has gone in on the other side. These ones often have two engines.

The war is still happening; even here, a long way from Sussex. One day three planes fly low over the hill above Bowns Green. I have seen them in my picture books, but never in real life. They are biplanes, clumsy looking things with two layers of stumpy wings. I think they are Gloster Gladiators. They follow the hill road, diving down towards Milford, and vanish over the curve of the hill. A few days later, Auntie Gladys has made us a picnic tea; and we are sitting in Redfearns field, above the stairway down into the village, when an amazing thing happens. There is a roaring sound of planes flying at full speed. Then from up the river come three big four-engined Lancaster bombers, flying only just above the water. One by one they pass below us, and we are looking down right into the cockpits. One of the pilots looks up at us waving: his mask is hanging loose, and he smiles broadly and waves back at us on the hillside. At the bend in the river below the village they rise slightly to our height, to clear the woods, then they vanish southwards from our sight. Long after this happened, I realised that this was probably the famous 617 Dam Buster squadron, keeping up their low-flying skills which made the famous raids on the Mohne and Eider dams last year.

House-Guests

It is autumn now, chilly and damp. Our sunny summer in Derby has faded into memory, and I am back at home, and school again. The Allied armies are advancing across France as far as the Rhine. And now we have different workers coming in the maroon bus to help on the farm - Germans. They do not seem to be monsters at all. Several of them speak a little English, and they are useful hands on the farm. They get paid a small amount for their work, which they can use for extra food or cigarettes. Really they work because it is more interesting than staying in the camp. Simon loves having gangs of men around, and makes them very welcome. Sherry is much more reserved, and watches them suspiciously. As with the Italians before them, my mother serves the same food as we are having for the midday meal. Meat of any kind is pretty scarce by now, the best is naturally reserved for the troops. My father is a handy shot with his double-barrelled twelve bore, and there are plenty of rabbits on the farm. One day I get back from school to find a distinct tension at home. It seems my mother had served up a really tasty rabbit stew for lunch, with garden-fresh onions. There were compliments to the cook, and the Germans asked what the meat was? When they understood they were eating rabbit there was an outburst of anger - as if we had served them rat meat! My father had to phone the camp to collect them early, with extra guards.

Squadron 617, Lancasters over Milford

The Quiet Land

My mother is quite a short person. She has short curly dark hair framing a rather round face, usually with an amused expression and sometimes with a positively impish smile. The most striking feature is a sometimes fierce look of determination in her eyes; once her course is set, she always gets her way. She was educated at home during the various farm moves. Beyond the skills that all farm people acquire, she trained as an artist and illustrator of childrens books. She is devoted to my father, who is a few years younger. He is a bit above average height, also with curly dark hair. He has a long oval face, with calm deep-set eyes, and a nose that seems to become more aquiline every year. He is generally restrained and patient with everyone, even under provocation, and he has a talent for persuading people to his point of view. Occasionally he smokes a pipe, which makes him look even more patient and thoughtful. They both work very long hours, as any stock farm is working from six in the morning till dark, or at least eight on summer evenings. So they often look weary.

Now that the camp is almost empty, our mother sometimes takes us for walks down in Possingworth Park. There is a long slope below the camp, where there are wild azaleas growing in what was once an elegant private park. There are several great Redwood Cedars there, with huge branches sweeping low above banks of pine needles. Rosemary and I learn to climb trees here: you can simply step up from branch to branch, like climbing a natural spiral staircase. One evening we are walking home holding hands on each side of mother, when we all notice a strange golden glow spreading round us. We turn around. A fantastic light is reaching out from the sun, sinking behind the Downs far to the south-west over Chanctonbury Ring. Glowing red-gold fire in the middle, it shades gently outwards and upwards into gilt and rose on the underside of the clouds overhead, until they too seem to catch fire, and the whole sky lights up with shreds of flame. We watch spell-bound, until the sun has long vanished, and slowly it draws the whole amazing spectacle after it into the west. Mother squeezes our hands, and says "I think that is the sunset we will remember all our lives". And we turn silently, and walk home. The oast-house cowl is still glowing a dusty pink as we cross Warren Lane.

My seventh birthday is on a cool grey day. There is almost nothing to buy in the shops, but my present is a pair of football boots and I am delighted with them. Mother has prepared a special birthday tea, and a birthday cake with real icing that she has saved up for months. We have just sat down to eat, when there is a knock on the front door. Obviously it is a stranger, as everyone who knows us comes to the kitchen window. I go to the door. There stands a stiff army officer, smiling a little awkwardly under his trim military moustache. "Can you tell me if there is a cafe up in the next village?" he asks. We say that there is only a tea-room, and at the weekend it is probably shut. He frowns, a bit disappointedly, and sets off up the road. After a moment, I say "He seems so lonely. Can't we invite him to tea?" Mother agrees immediately. So I run after him, and that is how we meet Captain Ian Ventris. He is very good company, and seems delighted to be with a real family and eating home cooking. It emerges later that his life has given him very little of either, as he is an only son and both his parents have died. He had been with the first wave of paratroops on D-Day. Now he is at the camp, re-forming a new company from the survivors, and training new recruits. Soon he is demonstrating parachute landings - flying down the stairs and rolling the length of the hall. Mother has to persuade him to stop, or he will crash right through the old floorboards! Ian becomes a firm friend, and often spends part of his leave with us. In truth, he doesn't really have any other home to go to. Before the end of the war he is a major, and has won the MC for gallantry in action.

The Windmill,
Cross-in-Hand

1945

The End of the War

Although in the middle of the winter the news on the BBC sounds worried, with the Germans resisting the Allies in Northern France, everyone feels that Germany is almost finished. Air raids have almost stopped, although the siren goes off now and then, and a lone German plane is seen. Even the heavy growling sounds in the skies - full of circling bombers - seem to have diminished as the planes assemble further north. The winter is cold and cheerless; and although there is every reason for hope, nobody seems particularly happy. Giles in the Daily Express does cartoons of the German High Command officers, each with a little cloaked scythe of death on their shoulder. And the schoolboys sing

> *Roll along covered wagon, roll along.*
> *Hitler won't be in England very long,*
> *He'll be lying on the grass, with a trumpet up his arse,*
> *Roll along, covered wagon, roll along.*

Of course, this is for the playground, not for the teachers.

We have a regular worker now from the POW camp. His name is Heinz. He is only about eighteen, fair haired, and is learning English very quickly. Simon loves him, and everyone else likes him too. Simon always goes up the outside stairs to the oast-house loft, and from there onto the foodstore roof, to welcome the arrival of the camp bus in the mornings. Heinz is very worried about what will happen to his family in Germany, as the war rolls ever closer to them. But there is no way he can hear from them. The Red Cross can try to send his letters through Switzerland, but there are no replies.

In April we all see the famous photograph in the newspapers of the Allied soldiers shaking hands across a stream with the Russians, as they finally join up in eastern Germany. Now Berlin is surrounded, almost all of Hitler's army in Germany have surrendered, and only a few are fighting desperately to save their Führer. It is useless.

Waldron Church

Soon the BBC tells us that German radio has announced that Hitler is dead. Next day the news is that all his army throughout north Germany has surrendered to General Montgomery at Luneberg Heath, and all the rest have surrendered to Eisenhower. The war is over! And immediately the church bells start ringing. I have never heard church bells in all my life: they have been silent since the war started, as they were going to be rung as an alarm in case of invasion. Now the peals of the bells roll across the fields and the woods from Waldron church until late in the evening, and for most of the next day. When Paris was liberated last summer, people were dancing in the streets. Here the feeling is more of relief than joy. There are big services at the war memorials to give thanks, and to remember those who died. And there is a general determination that, somehow, Germany must never be allowed to start another war. Next weekend in Robertsbridge there is a bonfire party, with even a few fireworks that have somehow survived the war. I watch them pop and flare in the light drizzle that is falling, and I wonder - is this it? Was this what it was all for? The war was certainly the most important thing in everybody's life; and it has been going on since my memories began. Now it seems to be ending, quite literally, like a damp squib in the Robertsbridge water-meadows.

Of course, although it was the war closest to us, this is VE day, for Victory in Europe. But the war is not yet ended, as Japan is still fighting on, and the British in Burma and the Americans in the Pacific Islands still have soldiers at war.

Heinz is still with us. The German soldiers have mostly been sent back to whatever awaits them at home - if they have one. Heinz comes from Potsdam, in the Russian zone, and no-one knows what they want. But the War Ministry wants to close the POW camp, so Heinz moves into the Big Room and lives with us. Eventually word comes that he is to be returned. There are sincere farewells, and he promises to write to us when he can. Simon waits sadly on the foodstore roof every morning for months, hoping he will return. But we never hear another word: Soviet communism swallows him, as it does so many others.

There are some almost unbelievable photographs in the papers from German concentration camps. But somehow, like the bombing damage on both sides, it is part of the horror of the war. It is going to take years for the monstrosity of what was done there to sink into peoples' minds.

In the early weeks of August there is more news from Japan. America has dropped a huge bomb on Hiroshima, which has destroyed the entire city. Two days later the same happens to Nagasaki. Next day Japan surrenders, and the Americans move in to liberate the starving prisoners of war. Now finally it is VJ day, and the war is really over.

Simon waiting...

Peace, and the Landscape Changes

My father takes Rosemary and me back to Derby for a holiday, to give our mother a bit of a break. Since we know the area now we enjoy showing him around. Uncle

Eric is showing him the mill works, which we have already seen. Except there is something we knew nothing about. He pulls a cover off a big barrel, which comes up through the floor, and says to Dad "Take a sniff of that". Incautiously, Dad puts his head in. I can still see him now, reeling back gasping. Uncle Eric is smiling knowingly - it was full of ammonia! Dad takes the 'joke' in good part, and we too thought it was a laugh. But at the end of my school career I do the same thing by accident - and it isn't funny!

When we arrive home again some things have already started changing. The first thing is that, one by one, all the signposts of England are being put back in their places. Every county has its own type of signpost. But the Sussex ones are special: they are made of wood, with an octagonal post and a matching overlapping black cap, like a French beret. They look very smart in their fresh white paint with black signwriting. One day I notice a ship out in Pevensey Bay: it isn't moving, and at night you can see the slow flash of a light from where it is anchored. The Royal Sovereign Lightship has come back. It is more than twenty miles from the farm; but sometimes with an east wind on a foggy day you can faintly hear a mournful lowing from its horn. People call it 'The Cow in the Channel'. Later a strange outline figure appears on the Downs, just before the fold round to Eastbourne. The Long Man of Wilmington is the outline of a man four hundred feet tall, cut through the short turf to the naked white chalk below. He is holding a long pole in each hand; an enigmatic design from the flint men of the Iron Age, before even Julius Caesar came to Britain. It had been covered up, to avoid the Luftwaffe using it to position themselves for their strafing raids on the coastal towns. But now it has re-emerged to keep its millenial watch over the Vale of Sussex. Nobody knows what it really signifies. But the schoolboys assure each other that it is a memorial to a blind hermit, who fell into a nearby chalkpit and died.

Cars are beginning to re-appear on the roads again. There is very little petrol for anyone, but you can have some - it isn't just for essential services. Pither's Garage in the village suddenly blossoms with fancy illuminated signs on its four petrol pumps. Dad says "It's just for show. It says Shell and BP and Fina and National Benzole - but it's just pool petrol in the tanks". Still, it makes the village look more cheerful. But the cars, which had been stored away for the war, are objects of fascination for a young boy. There are so many makes to learn about, famous names from our engineering heritage. As well as everyday Austins Fords and Morrises there are also Hillmans and Talbots, superior Singers Sunbeams and Standards, sporty MGs SSs and Jaguars, stately Lanchesters and Daimlers, boring Humbers, elegant Wolsleys and Vauxhalls, classy Alvises and Rileys, thundering Bentleys and silent Rolls Royces. They all have their own special badges you have to learn to recognise; some have famous histories as racing cars, like Bentleys. Some have legends like Rolls, and some have other notable things; like the strange whine of the Rileys and Lanchesters with their special Wilson gearboxes. There is so much for a young boy to learn about! And, in a garage at the Wheelrights in Heathfield lives the most fabulous monster of all: a sparkling scarlet Pontiac convertible of unimaginable size, with silver exhaust pipes coming out of the bonnet and plunging down into the wings. Just looking at this feast for the eyes, I feel that life has charms I had never imagined before.

And then, just when things are looking up, comes the shock. Suddenly, in spite of having led Britain to victory in the war, Winston Churchill is thrown out as prime minister in a General Election. My parents are horrified. My mother says "Oh, the socialists are treacherous swine. While he was winning the war and saving their necks, they were working to defeat him." My family is quite clear about political right and wrong. Merry England is not going to be restored. All big companies are taken away from their owners. Rationing does not end, but soon the rations get yet smaller. Taxes go up to pay for more planners and inspectors, and suddenly people realise that not only are the wartime regulations not over, rather they are getting worse. "That is how socialism works" says my father. "They tell you what you have to do, rather than letting you just do it. And because they have never done these things themselves, they get it wrong. So everyone gets poorer - except the 'experts' in the Ministries."

Harvest Home

But the farm must work: seven days a week the stock must be fed, and the growing herd of cows must be milked. One day at the end of September there is great excitement in the farmyard: the threshing team has arrived! The farm gate is opened wide, and in comes a steam traction engine, slowly pulling a big pink threshing machine up through the yard to its place beside the stacks of corn sheaves. The traction engine pulls away and turns slowly around to face the threshing machine, and a big driving belt couples the two machines together. The driver stokes up the fire, and then with a soft chuffing sound the belt starts to turn, steam and sulphurous coal smoke mingle and blow into everyone's faces, and with a strange wom-wom-womming sound, fans blowing and belts whirling, the threshing machine begins its work. Dad and our men, and several I have never seen before, are working like souls possessed. They strip the stack of corn sheaves down from its carefully laid roof, throwing the sheaves first down, then across, and finally up to the top platform of the thresher. Two men with knives rapidly cut the binder-twine, and throw the oats or wheat down into the flails of the thresher drum. The womming sound slows briefly as the machine digests its new mouthful, a pile of loose straw blows out from the back of the machine and falls to the ground, the chaff from the ears of the corn blows away on the wind and the draught from the powerful fans, and the golden grain pours out of chutes along the side into big hundredweight sacks of rough jute and sisal. The sacks of corn are carried away carefully; for this really is the harvest, the end result of ten or more months of painstaking work. By evening, with only half an hour's pause for sandwiches and huge drafts of tea, two corn stacks have been threshed to straw and grain; and the traction engine and its threshing machine puff ponderously away into the dusk for their next job. Next day the straw is gathered up under cover, or into other straw stacks in the open, to be used as bedding for the cows in winter. In long winters it is chopped up small and used to extend the hay ration for the cows. They may not like it, but a cow has to eat a barrowload of whatever it can get every day.

Threshing Time

The Green Bottle

The cupboard under the stairs is painted in simulation wood graining. If you look carefully at the grain lines, you can see that the painter faintly traced the word Robin near the top of the door. Inside the cupboard on a fairly high shelf is a dark green bottle; it has a white label with printed handwriting on it. Now I can reach the bottle, and I am curious. So I take it down, unscrew the top, and take a tiny sip. The first taste is rather nasty, so I swallow it quickly. Then a strange thing happens. Everywhere the stuff went, across my tongue and down my throat, a sudden warm glow spreads out, and lasts for about a minute. That was nice, I think. Curiosity satisfied, I put the bottle back. But next day I take another sip. After several days I decide to take more than one sip, and I have five or six. It feels lovely!

I go outside, and go for a ride on my bicycle. But it won't seem to behave, and it keeps swooping across the road in wild curves. I am puzzled about this - it has never done it before. Mrs Hall says to my mother later "Robin passed me on his bike this afternoon, and gave me the most angelic smile."

Next day, the bottle has gone.

The Pit

Down at the bottom of Warren Lane you can find the old entrance to the park. There is a lovely avenue of big lime trees. The army has cut parking places under the trees to hide their lorries. All the leaves have fallen, so there is no camouflage now. But the army and their lorries have all gone, and the avenue is deserted.. Below the lime avenue are the rifle ranges. At the top end behind the targets there is a steep bank of sticky yellow clay, to stop the rifle bullets. And in front of the targets there is a deep water-filled pit, which provided the clay. We have been playing around the ranges and along the edge of the clay-pit. Rosemary's boot sticks in the squelchy mud, she overbalances, and falls sideways into the yellow water. She vanishes completely except for her long ringlets of hair, which are floating on the surface. I reach out as far as I can, grab hold of her curls, and haul her out again: filthy, soaked to the skin, and spluttering muddy water from mouth nose eyes and ears. They say 'A Special Providence watches over drunks and small children'. Neither of us can swim. And, in the innocence of childhood, neither of us has any appreciation of the tragedy that nearly overtook us both. We are only worried about whatever our mother will say about the filthy clothes! We tip the water out of our gumboots, and set off home.

*Scythe, Swap
and Billhook*

Local Folk

At the kitchen window a man in a cloth cap is talking to Mother. "Oi come for the urrrrr." "Oh", says Mother, carefully, "which urrrr is that then?" "Yew know, the urrrrr wot you rented." "I didn't know we rented an urrrrr, when was that?" "Somewhen las' month." "What's it for?" "Yew arf-sharp, or summat? Yew pulls it across the fiels, after'n yew'm ploughed 'em!" "Oh - that urrrr" says Mother, relieved. "You'll find it down beside the Longshed." The man loads the harrow onto his trailor, and drives off.

Up the hill below the farm a strange figure is approaching, pushing his bike and balancing a large battered suitcase on the crossbar, calling on the five neighbours who live opposite our Longfield. He stops at our front gate, unloads the case, and brings it up to the porch. My mother says "Hello; we haven't seen you for years". He opens his case, and inside there is a profusion of things that haven't been seen in the shops for years either - lengths of lace, scarlet ribbons, expensive creams and lavender scented soaps, a few pairs of silk and nylon stockings, fine Moroccan leather gloves, and suchlike. Mr Old-Man, as I call him, is a travelling pedlar, and one of the last of his kind. Mother allows herself to be tempted to some lavender soap - she has a weakness for lavender. "I don't really need it", she says to me; "but he works so hard you feel you have to buy something". Mr

Old-Man, bald head perspiring in the sun, folds his jacket over the handlebars, lifts his heavy case onto the crossbar, and pushes his load onwards up the hill. "Before the war" says Mother "we used to have Spanish onion sellers. They came from Bilbao on the ships to Newhaven, and they walked around the country with strings of onions on poles across their shoulders till they were all sold. They were sweeter than English onions - they tasted almost like young apples." She looks wistfully down the road. But the onion sellers never come back.

Mary Durrant comes past with the milk trap, drawn by a patient pony. The milk trap is a special little cart with a low floor, where an elegant tall conical milkchurn stands in front of the driver. The Durrants have a dairy farm down the Under-Road on the way to Waldron, and they supply fresh milk to most of the people along our road. We only need it when our cows are dry, which is rarely these days. Mary is a cheerful soul, and engaging until you see her smile: she has appalling teeth. It is a common problem here in the Weald, where the ironstone water is too soft to provide calcium. We have special fizzy calcium pills, for the good of our teeth. The Durrants are a Sussex family from time out of mind. An older sister Edie keeps house for her widowed father. There are also two silent brothers. They are the local untouchables, who pump out the septic tanks into large wagons drawn by huge drayhorses. They don't speak much, and nobody has much to say to them. The whiff from the cess-carts is atrocious in summer. I once saw father Durrant, sitting by the kitchen range in midsummer dressed in an old smock and smoking a blackened clay pipe: he looked filthy and unimaginably old. I don't think any of his children married.

I learned in school, and in Kipling's stories, that Sussex was the centre of iron-founding in England long before the industry moved to Northumberland. The little rhyme goes

> Mr Huggett and his man John,
> They did make the first cannon.

Along the High Weald, deep in the woods, old ironstone pits are more common than the chalkpits on the Downs. The charcoal burners supplied the fuel to melt the iron, and the woods provided the brushwood for the charcoal and timbers for the ships. The streams are stained with the brown algae which are nourished by the dissolved iron in the water.

> See you the little lane that runs
> Among the dappled wheat?
> Oh that was where they hauled the guns
> That smote King Phillip's fleet.

It is strange to think that in Elizabethan times rural Sussex was the industrial heart of our England. The old names, the Durrants, Huggetts, Hooks, Honeysetts and Hobdens, have lived and farmed and toiled here since before records began.

Penny

Penny has her third birthday this summer, and is quietly beginning to assert her independence. It is not easy always being the youngest. Certainly you get looked after: but everyone else does the choosing for you. Penny started speaking quite late, when she was nearly two. Her speech is also rather strange: her consonants are frequently different, and she stubbornly will not be corrected. So Rosemary becomes shortened to Nonie; she refers to herself as Nenny, or Mnepoly when given in full. Telephone becomes Polypo, and so on. Rosemary and I understand her well enough, but visiting family find it rather hard going. It is about this time that Dr Cuddiford listens to her thoughtfully, then produces a little light and looks in her ears: they are completely blocked with hard wax, and have been so since one of her many fevers. When this is washed away, her interesting pronunciations are gradually abandoned. But oddly enough the names she gave people and things remain as family parlance; Rosemary is Nonie for ever.

The Common

Opposite Mrs Hall's house is a wild place we call the Common, running up from Brown's Lane to the top of the hill. Cattle sometimes graze there, but mostly it is over-run with gorse bushes, bracken and brambles. In early summer the gorse bushes are a blaze of gold blossom that gives off a heady 'green' perfume. Here

A Sussex Trug

Mother teaches us to recognise yellow-hammers and goldfinches, tree creepers, and all the other brightly coloured birds that hide in the undergrowth. At summer's end we gather trugfuls of blackberries; to make puddings, and jams for the winter. Here we children play hide and seek; we know every path and passage through the bushes. But in five acres of bushes even we sometimes cannot find a successful hider. So then we call in the dogs: "Ha loss Penny, Simon!" "Go fetch Nonie, Mitch." (Mitch is Penny's pronunciation of bitch, which she once heard applied to Sherry. It sticks.) Once he catches onto the idea, Simon is very quick at tracking people. For Sherry, it all seems too much like work: she is really rather lazy. That is, until she gets riled - then everyone had better watch out!

Goldfinch

The Seaside

It is a big treat - Grannie Brown is taking us to the seaside. Rosemary and I catch the bus from the farm gate to Hailsham, where Gran now lives. From the village you can catch a bus to the four corners of the county every hour, or even every half hour at times. The pale green Southdown and the dark green Maidstone buses provide transport for about a penny a mile, and it is no hardship not to have a car - you can still go anywhere. We sit in front on the top deck, and play spotting games - like counting the number of ponds, or horses. Then Gran takes us on to Eastbourne. The beach has only recently been re-opened to the public, after the minefields have been cleared. We don't have swimming costumes, so there is nothing much to do except sit on the sloping shingle beach and eat our picnic. The beach boats are offering rides out to Beachy Head lighthouse, but I think Gran is nervous of the sea. So I go exploring out on the groyne, one of the wooden breakwaters that run down to the sands at low tide to stop the shifting of the shingle. The pebbles are quite high on one side, while the waves run foaming past on the other side. I climb over, step on a wet wooden beam - and suddenly I am under water with my eyes still open, looking amazed at the white bubbles swirling in the green sea as I spin over and over, with nothing to hold onto. Out of nowhere a hand grabs my shirt, and hauls me up over the groyne: I was rescued by a man I never clearly saw, and returned to a mortified Gran. The day at the seaside comes to an untimely end with me, wringing wet, huddled over the radiator at the front of the bus, which is turned on specially by the kindly conductor.

The Stage

Our village of Cross-in-Hand is putting on a Variety Show. It is the event of the season. There is a scene from the Midsummer Night's Dream, about the transformation of Bottom into an ass. Rosemary is dancing Fairy Mustardseed. This is more appropriate than had been imagined when someone goes to lift her down from the stage, and is told in ringing tones "Take your filthy hands off me!" Some fairies are not to be trifled with - then or since! Two black minstrels are introduced under exotic names as guest artists: a frail old man is singing Old Black Joe; and accompanying him another, sitting cross-legged on the floor, is playing a tenor banjo. I am captivated by the sentimental tune and the strange plangent sound of the instrument. After a while though, something seems familiar about the singer. Slowly under the black make-up I recognise my friend Joe the roadman. I chat regularly with him on the way home from school, as he chops and lays the blackthorn hedges, or cuts the grass with a swap -the local name for a sickle. Looking more carefully now at the banjo player I see Mr R.Q.Clarkson, the postmaster. Well, well. But the star of the show is a real visiting artist, and a famous one at that. Ralph Richardson, who was born in Burwash up the road, is singing a broad and saucy Sussex version of Villikins and his Dinah.

Now our Sary went milikin' with Nellie the cow.
She tugged and she pulled, but 'er did'n quite know 'ow.
Till after a while Nellie turned with a frown;
Sayin' "You 'ang on toight, love, an' Oi'll jump up an' down!"

One day when my Sary were milkin the cow,
The stool overbalyanced, and she fell some'ow.
" 'Ave you 'urt yourself badly?" I started to yell.
She cried "Oi've 'urt my ar--m", but that worn't where she fell!

Our Village

Cross-in-Hand seems an odd name for a village, even in a Christian country, if you haven't lived with it for your whole life. People say it was where an army camped on its way to embark on one of the Crusades. Likewise the next village down the Lewes road, Blackboys, was where they returned with their captured Nubian slaves. It consists of a double line of small shops along the road which slopes below the windmill on its hilltop. At the bottom is a junction by the Baltic Sawmills, where the whine of the saws and the smell of cut pine is carried along with the smoke from the panting steam engines. We have a pub and Pithers Garage, an ironmonger, an outfitters shop, The Post Office, The Handy Stores, a blue-tiled butchers shop and Wooleys the greengrocers. This little centre supplies everyone's domestic needs for a few miles around. The smart houses are mostly down Back Lane; and Beaconsfield Terrace, down the Waldron Road towards our farm, houses the less well-heeled of our community. We have our own bootmaker and cobbler at the top of Waldron Road. And at the bottom end of the Terrace, Smith combines several trades: he services the soles and heels of our shoes that are worth repairing, and he also cuts our hair. We sit on a high stool, and the cut hair falls among the leather trimmings beside his shoemakers lasts. He also repairs pots and pans. Along Warren Lane, halfway to Blackboys, is a line of really smart houses built by the Lyons Green company along the edge of Possingworth Park. Opposite them Miss Rolls, an heiress of the Rolls-Royce founder, lives in chauffered and butlered elegance. And in a tiny shop in Warren Lane, with a large family of girls, Mr Jupp's bakery bakes the most delicious crusty Hovis bread. He also does malty currant loaves, and hot cross buns for special occasions. When the weather is dry we walk there across the fields; and in the wet we slip through the Twitten, which is a narrow path bordered by garden hedges between the two roads.

Behind the pub, which likes to think of itself as The Cross-in-Hand Hotel, is a small village hall. Here my mother sometimes gives dancing lessons to the growing tribe of children of the village. After all, we will soon be going to parties, and then dances, and we will have to know how to dance properly. So we learn the waltz and the quickstep; but much more to our taste we also learn the traditional country dances - Square Dances, Highland Reels, Gay Gordons, Strip the Willow, to say nothing of the older ballroom dances like the Valeta, the Polka, the St Bernards Waltz, the Palais Glide and the Conga. It is all great fun. We may be a farming community, but our parents have not forgotten the elegance of the years between the wars, and they have high social hopes for us.

1947

The Endless Winter

At first it seems enjoyable. We have a White Christmas, and then more snow in January. And February. And March. Rosemary and I take the heavy farm sledge - which my father had built during his own schooldays - across to the steep slope in Browns Lane which runs down to the bridge over the stream, which is a headwater of the River Cuckmere. From the end of school to the early winter dusk we are down there sledging in the wet snow. But hot toast, with dripping and Bovril, is calling us. Then we drag the sledge homewards, and warm ourselves up in front of the coal fire in the sitting room. But it is not that easy. Our numbed hands and feet hurt and sting as the blood slowly flows back: it is the dreaded 'hot-ache'. And where it hurt most on our heels and ankles, the red cracked welts of chilblains appear. Other things start going wrong too. One morning the Waldron bus skids on the hill above us. The tyres cannot hold it, and it slides slowly backwards until it falls at an alarming angle into the ditch. The driver and conductor sit by our kitchen stove for most of the morning, until a towing truck rescues them and the bus. The bus service stops. I see a Bren-Gun Carrier on the road skid on its tracks through nearly a full circle, and end in the hedge. Then, when spring is expected, comes the fog. It lies over everything, a freezing grey cloud. At first the trees and hedges grow crystals, and look quite pretty even in the gloomy light. But the telephone wires grow such thick layers of ice that eventually the copper breaks under the weight. Slowly the telephone system in the countryside breaks down almost completely. It is well into April before the thaw sets in. And then come the floods, as three months of collected snow starts to melt. Each little stream becomes a torrent. The rivers cannot cope; they burst their banks, and the Vale of Sussex becomes a lake.

During the Easter holidays I go again to stay with my Mother's family in Robertsbridge. It is a fascinating place for a young boy who loves water. The bridge was built by Archbishop Robert sometime in the twelfth century, when the Normans were running England. It consists of about five separate bridges linked by a causeway across the Rother Valley, and they cross all the wandering branches of the River Rother and the River Dudwell, which flood most winters. But this year is special. The water spreads right across the valley, and in it five whirling currents mark the little riverbeds course through the fields. On the far side is McDougal's Flour Mill, a big building which spans the main river, and has a watermill in the foundations. The roof is covered with big finned ventilator cowls - a bit like huge tin turkey heads.

Opposite the mill is the little village of Salehurst, where my parents were married, as it was my mother's parish church. Robertsbridge is a very pretty village: most of the houses are built of white plaster and black half-timbers, and many of them have thatched roofs too. The fire wardens had a hard job keeping it safe during the air raids. An incendiary bomb could have taken half the village.

The water not needed by the mill falls with a frightening roar into the mill pit, and then away down a branch of the river which has been deepened, and now is called the Tank Trap. If you can't swim you have to be pretty careful around here. I can't swim. And even if you can swim, I don't know what chance you would have during the floods. I walk out onto a footbridge lower down the stream; it is a spindly structure on long wooden poles. I look down to the rushing muddy water in the Tank Trap below, and suddenly I realise that the whole bridge is drumming with the force of the current. Carefully, I walk back, and pick my way beside the torrents, and through the flooded fields to the farm. "Oh, there you are" says Granny Bonfield; "lunch is ready". Children can come and go as they please in the holidays.

The Lord Mayors Show

It is a grey day at the end of spring, and I have gone to play with Ian Maitland, who lives near Burwash on a hillside above the Rother valley. The treat is that Television is beginning again. They have a TV set from before the war, and everyone gathers round to look at this little box, like a little grey cinema. It is showing an endless grey procession of tanks and guards on horseback; it is raining in London too. We quickly stop paying attention, and go outside to play boats in the overflowing ditches running down the hill to the river. My interest in television lasts less than fifteen minutes, and never returns.

Mud and Providence

Possingworth Lake has been drained. The owners of the park are trying to restore some of its former elegance, and they know something we did not. It is in fact an artificial lake, made by a little earth dam across a shallow valley with a stream running through it. And the makers put a drain at the middle. Nicolas and I look in awe at this expanse of yellow-grey mud: we can see things out there that look interesting. But when we try walking out to look, we sink up to our knees in the mud. I have an idea. One of my books has pictures of Canadian trappers wearing snowshoes: can we make some mud-shoes? We go back to Nicolas's house, and spend the afternoon cutting out plywood rectangles; threading binder-twine through holes so it can tie over our boots. They drag a bit, but they stay on when we test them on the lawn. Next morning we go down again to the lake, and try them out. Nonie comes along to watch, a bit annoyed that we haven't made any for her. At one point my mudshoes stick, and slowly they sink in the mud. I cannot pull them out, and I can't reach to untie them either. Nonie struggles out through the mud, and reaches down to untie the twine for me. Then we go to look for the things, lying on the bottom of the lake. Shiny brass cylinders, with pointed lead cones at one end: I know them from pictures - they have to be canon shells. There are mortar bombs too. We build a small collection on the bank. The Canadian soldiers had dropped them in the lake to kill the goldfish. One of them starts bubbling slightly when I wipe the mud off it. Our Possingworth Special Providence must have been working overtime! We leave them there on the bank: Nicolas takes one of the canon shells home to show his father. Providence relaxes again, perspiring slightly. Just as we sit down to lunch, an almighty explosion shakes every window for miles, and breaks them all in the Possingworth Hotel. A German landmine, destabilised by the draining of the water, has destroyed half of an island in the lake.

School Again

I am standing in the dry ditch on the far side of our hill, and thinking that, if it weren't for the large crop of wild strawberries on the bank above me, life would be rather hard. At school the horseplay is getting very tough. The playground in break is the scene of frequent fights. When I mention this to Mother, she is not very sympathetic. "Stick up for yourself then: hit them back!" Well, this morning I land a blow on the jaw of Peter Lall: his look of surprise made it worth the other bruises. Still, I have an ally, who is big for his age and can use his weight. Andrew becomes my best friend. I find friends are very useful at times. Mother also says that I have to pull my socks up at lessons, as in four years I will have to take the Common Entrance Exams to go to boarding school. Grazing steadily on the wild strawberries, I think suddenly that four years is not forever. I can remember starting at Tavistock, and that was more than four years ago. Like many children, I live in a permanent 'today'. Until that afternoon, this term is forever; and then this holiday is forever too. But somehow they end. Suddenly I wake up to the passing of time: these four years will end too. If I do not make an effort I will disappoint my parents; and while school work is mostly tiresome I think it is preferable to that. In a relatively small school the classes are flexible, and as boys leave at the top and we move up, somehow I find myself grouped with boys who are mostly a year older than me.

Mr Bucknall, the original Headmaster, has handed the school on to Mr Ward. The school becomes a family affair in a way. Mrs Ward is the eldest daughter of a large Irish family, the Magners. And all her sisters become the staff, Miss T runs the kitchens, Miss A is the nurse, Miss J runs the laundry, and so on down the line. Mrs Ward teaches all the languages, English, French, and Latin too. She is strict on discipline: woe betide you if homework is delivered late. But there are compensations. Reading the accounts in Latin of how two thousand years ago the Caesars conquered an Empire which included our own island nation is quite fascinating. We admire the Romans, as we also have an Empire to run - an Empire on which the sun never sets. When I grow up, my future is clear. I think it came from readings of Hackluyt's Book of Voyages on the radio. I will join the Navy, and voyage all round the world protecting our Empire. The Navy seems rather like a school in fact. Someone is always senior to everyone else; everyone has nicknames, and it is only for boys - and men too of course. The Navy even has its own schools and colleges. For all my schooldays this is my only ambition. You only need one.

The School Camp

Tavistock organises a school camp at the beginning of the summer holidays. We are all taken down to Magham Down, to a field just at the inland edge of the Pevensey Marshes. We camp on blankets in ex-army bell tents. We lie there at night, with the door flaps open to the afterglow of sunset, and then to the stars, and we tell each other ghost stories until we fall asleep. By day we eat half-cooked sausages heated over an open wood fire. And we bathe naked in the drainage canals amid the mud and the bulrushes; and we are gloriously happy. Until one day, when the masters in charge decide to take us to the seaside. This is a walk that takes all morning until early afternoon. There is a steep shingle bank down to the sea at Pevensey Bay, and those of us who can make the effort can walk down and paddle our sore feet in the Chops of The Channel. Then we walk back again. Six miles in each direction, in beating sunshine, on roads of chipped flint and melting tar. There is no shade on the marshes, hardly a single tree. We are too exhausted to eat supper. Most of our thin plimsols are worn to shreds.

My Brother, Friends, and God

At the end of the holidays my brother is born. And while having a brother should be fun, I am almost ten and there is no way we are going to be close companions.

I suppose that my mother rather senses this. Perhaps hoping to foster some brotherly feeling, she asks me to choose his names. So I suggest Andrew, after my best friend at school; and Patrick because I like the name. As he grows up Patrick is the label he prefers, and the name Andrew is abandoned.

The Lytchgate, Waldron Church

I no longer see so much of my friend Nicholas, as he goes to a different school. His family are Catholics, so they have to go to Catholic schools to learn about different morals and a rather different God. Catholics believe they will go to Hell if they go to ordinary schools, or marry people who aren't Catholics. At least that is what the Nuns teach them. Sussex doesn't like Catholics very much. Bloody Queen Mary had nine local people burned alive at the stake in Lewes market square, for simply wanting to read the Bible in English. For the Catholics that was heresy. Sussex people know there are oaks still standing in the deep woods that were already grown trees when it happened: people here are slow to forgive, and they never forget.

Meanwhile our Mother decides that a bit of godliness will do us no harm, and we are despatched after Sunday lunch every weekend to Sunday School. The list of Rectors at Waldron goes back to the year 1195, and our church replaced an older Saxon church. It is a beautiful Norman country church, set in a large graveyard of new and old headstones. All the local history for hundreds of years is here in the names on those stones,– birth, life, marriage, illness, death - and we absorb it all. As they were, so we will be. The heavy door closes with an echoing clunk behind us. The church clock strikes quarter to three: as the last chimes fade away the Reverend Percy Wilmot-Jenkins appears in his robes at the vestry door. "We will sing number 165 in Hymns Ancient and Modern; "Oh God, our help in ages past"." There is a sighing sound from the bellows as a silent youth pumps up the organ, and the little service begins. We pray for the health of the King, and for forgiveness for our sins - like cheating on school tests, I suppose. A dozen or so local children sing along; and we always end with "Jesu, lover of my soul". The rector hands out stamps to stick in our Sunday School album, where each page carries the text 'Every stamp says Duty Done: every blank cries Shame!' Then there is the long walk home. Penny rebels about the walk one Sunday. "Come on" says Rosemary, handing her a hazel switch, "let's play 'driving the pigs to market' ". "Alright" says Penny tartly, "You be pig, and I won't play!"

1948

Catching the Full-Toss

Mr Ward wants to get the season under way early, and so we are practising our cricket on the short eighteen yard pitch. It is a sunny March day, but the grass is still wet. I am batting. Geof Woodley, the school's fast bowler, runs up to bowl, and I see his freckled oval face looking slightly surprised as he slips. I can see the ball, new scarlet leather, about a foot in front of my face. Then there is a wrenching bone-splintering pain in my mouth as the ball smashes into it. I can taste and smell blood as it pours down my face and my shirt. I yell out, then clasp both hands across my mouth and run fast to the washrooms. I bend over the sink, and by the time the staff find me I have staunched the flow and dabbed my split lip to only a trickle. Probing my bleeding gum with my tongue I realise there is a gap. With sinking heart I look in the mirror: too true - one of my big front teeth, so recently acquired, has gone. It was crooked, but it was mine. Mr Vaughan, the maths teacher, comes in. "We found your tooth in the grass" he says, "and your mother says we must take you to your dentist." Mr Butcher, the dentist, washes the tooth in a little glass bowl, and then pushes it back into its bleeding socket. The rest of that week is a nightmare of pain. He takes an imprint of my front teeth, then he sticks my jaw closed with gutta percha and a tight bandage under my jaw and over my head. Next day he puts on a metallic tasting splint, to hold the tooth in place. Dr Cuddiford gives me a laughing gas anaesthetic. But he is nervous about giving gas to a child, and doesn't give me enough. I have to blow into a mouthpiece which makes a whistling noise. I go limp, but I can still hear them talking, and it hurts badly. For ages afterwards I have to drink soup and fruit puré through a tube .

Two years later, my gum has closed up around the tooth. Mr Butcher hopes for signs that the nerve has joined up - and he writes a research paper about it. But it is still wobbly, and I cannot really use it to bite anything like an apple.

The Folds

One of my jobs is locking up the folds. These are triangular wooden structures, with a little henhouse for about a dozen hens and a cockerel, and an outdoor hen-run covered with wire netting. We have lines of them across the meadows; they are moved every day so the chickens have fresh grass to eat, and the manure fertilizes the soil. My Dad has been worried for some time about hens disappearing. Farmers accept that poachers take a chicken here and there, but you cannot afford to lose too many. Rearing a hen and bringing it into lay takes seven months and costs a lot of feed and care: nothing grows for free on a farm. Now the losses are getting expensive. So my father rigs

Dad and the Folds

a system where a chain runs through the middle of the hutch between the two trapdoors, and at night we put a padlock through the chain. Poaching losses fall to nothing. Walking round the farm locking up with a flashlamp in the evening is good fun. On these trips my mother introduces me to the star constellations: the Plough and Orion in the winter sky, and a little plough overhead in the summer. Some people call the Pleaides the Seven Stars; country people here call them Dick-and-his-Wagon.

Village People

Most of the characters of the village live in Jubilee Terrace, at the top of Waldron Road just below Cross-In-Hand. There is a strange stooped person, the size of a boy, always dressed in shorts and a cloth cap and beetle-boots. He wheezes as he walks, muttering "Poor ol' 'Arry, mmnn"; but when you see his face you realise he must be over forty. He is one of Grandpa French's sons. People employ him to go on errands, post letters, and otherwise do small odd jobs. But the boys from the Terrace are very hard on Harry French, and bully him mercilessly.

Bumper Humphries is a tall man with a permanent stoop and a limping gait. He had TB, and was never called up for the army. He lives with his sister in the Terrace, and keeps a few hens in his back garden: he always has a dozen or so new born chicks to sell in the Heathfield or Hailsham markets every week. He seems to get surprisingly good hatches from his little flock. He is a good friend of PC Hill, our local rather ponderous village policeman: often late in the evening, or on the way to school in the early morning, you will meet them walking along the country lanes together.

Nightmare!

My bedroom has moved to the back of the house, looking out over the garden to the cowshed and two poultry houses. The cowshed is a solid brick structure. The poultry houses are the brooder house, where young chicks are reared, and the interim house where the older ones are kept before they go out to the fields. They are wooden built, and painted with creosote to prevent rot. The chicks are kept warm by little paraffin lamps to simulate the warmth of a mother hen, and they grow happily.

It must be late in the night. Something, some sound, has disturbed me. I listen: there is a sort of crackling noise. I open one eye. A vivid orange light is dancing on the wall opposite. I leap out of bed, and my worst wartime nightmare is happening before my eyes - the interim house is burning from end to end. Flames and sparks fly high into the air. I run in to wake my parents. But it is much too late, nothing can be done. An hour later, as a grey dawn is breaking, nothing remains but fifty yards of brick foundations. In the smouldering embers are hundreds of little carbonised corpses, incinerated alive. Mother says "That is a terrible blow. They were going to be raised as table birds for Christmas. Now we will have nothing to sell."

Normans Bay

This year our mother decides she can do a better job than Tavistock. She has experience, as she was a Wolf Cub Mistress before the war in Robertsbridge, and Akela took her pack camping. She shows us her Wood Badge, a treasured leather thong with some notched wooden toggles, awarded for woodcraft and camping skills. Then she produces photos of her Cub Pack, and wipes away a tear. "Why?" "Because most of those young boys became soldiers, and some didn't come back". So we go to a campsite behind the beach at Normans Bay, just along from Pevensey. Mother rents another bell tent for the family, and once again we camp out in the field. She takes a whole fortnight's supplies for us, and cooks over a primus stove. The results are much better than the school camp last year. I am allowed to take my friend Andrew along. For days we amuse ourselves catching crabs with bacon-rinds on string in the land drains. Or maybe by shrimping with small nets along the sands at low tide. Mother cooks our little collection of shrimps for us in salty water over the primus. The railway runs along beside the camp, and we lie outside the tent in the evening, watching the trains going between Hastings and Eastbourne, and on to London either way. Usually they have Pullman carriages, each with its own name on the side. Some special

Horse
Mushrooms

trains are all-Pullman, like the famous Brighton Belle. The passengers sit at dining tables with shaded lamps on them, shining in the dusk as the trains whisk them across the marshes. We think how rich these people must be, to be able to be so smart. Mother teaches us rounds and other tuneful songs she taught her cubs before the war - The Bells of Saint Mary's, Frère Jaques, The Long Long Trail, and so the evenings pass. One evening she takes us across the tracks, where the warning signs date back to The London Brighton and South Coast Railway, then across the fields to The Star Inn, a little white planked country pub all alone in the marshes. We sit at a table under the willows in the garden, as children are not allowed in bars. But this is where I am allowed to try cider, and ginger beer shandy, for the first time. Coming back across the meadows Mother spies something a little way off in the dewy grass: it looks like a cluster of pebbles. "Ah" she says, "horse mushrooms - how lovely". She slips her fingers under them and lifts them gently. "Look, underneath they are pink, and as they get older they will go brown. Never eat ones which are white underneath. And look" - she turns one over - "the top skin peels off easily, that's another sign of edible ones. I'll cook these for us tomorrow for breakfast." I remember the smell of those mushrooms frying with bacon in the misty morning for a long time.

Mother excels herself for Penny's fifth birthday. She has brought from home a lovely birthday cake. Weeks of carefully hoarded rations in flour and butter, sugar and currants, went into the cake mixture. Plenty of children from the campsite are invited to Penny's birthday tea. After a picnic lunch we all go down to the beach for a splash in the sea. When we come back, we are dumbfounded. The tentflap is hanging open, and the cake and most of our supplies have vanished! Mother is outraged: beyond the spoiled birthday party, most of our food for the rest of the holiday has gone. Mother sets off to complain to the village policeman. Suspicion quickly falls on a teenage youth in a nearby tent. After a search the cake, apart from a large missing slice, is restored for compassionate reasons, so Penny has her birthday party. But the stolen stores are held as evidence for several days. The neighbouring families raid their own modest surpluses to see us through. The youth, who had run away from London, is sent to Borstal. Justice in 1948 is swift and severe.

Dad comes down in the big Standard on the Saturday morning for the day. We want him to join in games and play on the beach. But he just smiles indulgently at us, sits down in a deck chair, and goes to sleep. Mother says quietly, "I think this is the first day-off he has taken since before the war."

Ian Goes Courting

Ian, our adopted Paratroop Major, usually spends some of his leave with us, if he is in England at all. He likes to see us all, chat with Dad, and take Simon out for walks. He has a series of motorbikes for getting around, each one more powerful than the last. The first is a Triumph Speed Twin, a hairy five hundred cc machine. This is followed by a Triumph Tiger 100, said to be capable of a hundred miles an hour. He goes off around the countryside, calling on various girl-friends. Sometimes he brings them back to the farm: they are usually not dressed for the motorbike, and are struggling with tight skirts and high heels. Sherry evidently disapproves of them - not having seen anything like that around the farm before. Usually Ian asks Mother what she thinks of them, and she usually replies "I'm not sure that she is really your type", or "Do you think she would like being a soldiers wife?"

The next bike is even more powerful; it is the famous Triumph Thunderbird. Ian asks Mother if he can take me on a visit to friends in Hawkhurst? Hawkhurst is about twenty miles away, just into Kent. So I climb on the pillion seat, hang on tight to Ian, and off we go. Ian is wearing a big duffle coat, and I cannot get my arms right round him - although I would like to - so I hang onto his coat pockets all through Heathfield, then the three Burwashes (Weald, Common, and plain Burwash). I have got the hang of balancing now, and I can hear what Ian is saying as neither of us have helmets. As we approach Etchingham I am not even holding on; and I am sitting there happy and quite relaxed as we come onto the famous Straight Mile, which is a section of an old Roman Road. Ian shouts over his shoulder "Okay, let's see what she will really do!"; he winds the throttle wide open, and suddenly he lies down flat on the petrol tank. I am hit in the chest by a ninety five mile an hour headwind, and I am knocked backwards on the saddle and almost blown away: somehow I just get a finger of each hand into Ian's duffle pockets. Providence has quick reactions.

This year Ian arrives in a bright red sports car. In fact the car is gutless, a Lloyd with a two stroke motor bike engine. Ian says "It's not much fun, but it looks good. An officer should have something a bit dangerous - if only for the morale of the troops!" But after a few expeditions he brings home Edna for lunch. She is a cheerful young woman with a slightly freckled face and a permanent smile, who immediately makes friends with both Sherry and Simon. "I'm used to dogs", she says, "I grew up with them"; and she settles to reading a story to Penny. After lunch, she automatically clears the table, and starts the washing up. Ian raises a questioning eyebrow at Mother. "Keep this one", she says with a smile.

Boarding School

Mother is seriously ill. She is taken to St Mary's Hospital in Eastbourne to have her gall-bladder removed. The gallstones are so big that this is the only way she can be cured, and the operation scar runs from her spine round to her navel. My poor mother is in St Mary's for almost three months, and the family is re-arranged. Dad's cousin Connie comes to stay as housekeeper, and to look after all the others. To reduce the load, I go to stay at Tavistock as a boarder for a while. It is a bit of a shock at first, not sleeping in my own bed. But you get used to a dormitory quite quickly, and at least there is company all the time. The main problem is school food. The supplies are strictly rationed, as Britain is broke. The meat ration goes down to eight pennyworth per week per person, but you are lucky if the butchers have any at all. And the Magner girls have plenty of Irish charm, but they are not talented cooks. Potatoes and chunks of swede are served boiled without salt - you cannot swallow it without gagging. One day with a cold salad I am given a slice of grey mutton: when I turn it over there are about forty white maggots crawling on the underside. It is exchanged for another one without livestock, but still inedible.

The saving grace is that on Sundays I can cycle home to have Sunday lunch, and see the family. One Sunday at the end of the autumn we are having lunch, and I am surprised to see our dog Simon sitting beside my father, and hopefully eyeing his plate. Our dogs have known since they were puppies not to pester for food at table. So I am even more surprised when Dad picks a choice morsel off his plate, and gives it to Simon, who swallows it gratefully. Eventually I ask why Dad is breaking his own rules? "He was poisoned last week". "What?!" Dad explains: "It looked as if he was having a fit - spasms and retching and foaming at the mouth. I have seen it before; this is not the first time it has happened. But this time I knew what to do. I mixed a lot of salt and warm water, and forced his jaw open enough to pour it in from a bottle. He was violently sick, and the poisoned meat came back. I called the vet, and he survived - just." My poor lovely Simon!! "But when did it happen before?" "We had two Great Danes when you were a baby. I kept them on a long chain to guard the folds at night: I was too late to save Sunny. I sent Susan away before the thief killed her too." So that was the very faint memory of a big dog, somewhere in my most distant past. "But what was it?" "Strychnine. It is sold as rat poison. It only needs a little on some meat thrown over the wall into the yard, or left in a field. It takes about twenty minutes of agony to kill a dog, or a person". "But who would do a thing like that?" "A poacher, probably" is all Dad will say.

But the dogs know. When certain footsteps go past on the road - step, drag, step, drag, - they growl, even in their sleep. The only food Simon will eat till next summer comes off my father's plate.

Grandparents

Granny Bonfield dies in the autumn. She was a lady with a very stern Victorian way of dressing and wearing her hair which demanded respect. But in fact she was quite flexible with us children, and a good cook. Grandpa Bonfield moves in to live with my Aunt Yoe in Robertsbridge. He appeared to be in good health, then only six weeks later he suddenly died. Someone says it was of a broken heart. I hadn't seen Grandpa for quite some time, and little was said about his dying: death is considered an unsuitable subject for children. But I was fond of him.

Modern History

Major Stone is an old soldier. He has one leg amputated above the knee; sometimes he winces at pain in the bit that is no longer there. He is supposed to teach us history. But he says it is happening while we speak. Although Britain helped America develop the atom bomb, we are building our own, and the first tests are being prepared in Australia. And Soviet Russia, so recently our ally, is trying to starve Berlin, so the famous airlift is just starting. Churchill's prediction of an Iron Curtain falling across Europe is coming true. Then the Korean War starts, and Britain and America and the Empire are at war again with communist China, this time with the United Nations in support. That was a bit of luck; the Soviets stormed out, and were not present at the only chance for a veto. But Major Stone says that won't stop them. "If we aren't at war with Russia by next year, then maybe they will back off, and settle for the half of Europe they already have. But we have no better than an even chance. Of course a lot of our socialists are communists at heart, and they don't want to believe ill of Russia even in spite of Berlin. But they are our government. So we are unprepared, and the Russians will probably win." Chamberlain's promise of 'Peace in our time' looks ever less likely to be our future.

1949

Milking Time

Dad brings the cows in for milking, early in the morning, and then at the end of the afternoon. A cow in milk gets uncomfortable if left for too long, so they are usually waiting at the gate, and walk willingly into the cowshed. Dad is wearing a long khaki overall, and a small skull cap that was once white - a long time ago. He puts some mash of cracked oats in each cow's feeder; as they stoop down to eat he closes the long metal slide around their necks. He washes the udders carefully with warm water, and with another pail he washes their back legs up to their tails. "Do you want to try milking?" he asks me. So I sit down on the little three legged stool: Daisy looks round in some surprise at this variation of routine. "You make a ring between finger and thumb, and you close them around the top of the teat, up close to the udder. Then you close your other fingers into the palm of your hand, and squeeze and pull down at the same time." So I do that, and a jet of warm milk squirts down into the pail with a tinkling sound. The smell is lovely, redolent of cows and calves and cream, with a strong scent of the grasses and flowers of the fields. I try with both hands. Daisy munches on contentedly. But after only a dozen or so squeezes my hands ache so much that I have to stop. It is much harder than it looks. Dad takes over again. Each cow takes about five minutes, and we have twelve. Each bucketful of milk is weighed, then poured into a churn. Later, in the scullery, the churn is emptied through a filter into a big funnel; and it runs slowly down over a cooler, which has cold water running through. If you don't cool the milk quickly, it goes sour before you get it to the dairy. After milking, everything - buckets and churns, and the cooler itself - must be carefully washed with detergent, then rinsed with fresh water. This is the rhythm, twice a day, every day of the year. Even with electric milking machines, dairy farming is very hard work.

Still, we love the benefits of having our own milk. Mother pours some of our milk into big settling pans, so that the thick yellow cream rises to the surface. This is skimmed off, and we churn most of it into our own golden butter. But we can have real cream with fruits from the garden. The government seems to be ruining the country in a hapless sort of way: some socialists and unionists campaign for the farms to be taken away and nationalised. "Our Land belongs to Our People". (By 'our', they mean workers in the cities) My father snorts that, if the only farmers are civil servants on a forty four hour week, the livestock of the country will be dead in a month! But meanwhile, some luxuries are the fruits of our own labours.

The Swimming Pool

In May Mr Ward decides that Tavistock should have a swimming pool. This is sunk into the old cricket pitch, where my tooth was knocked out. I think this is definitely a change for the better! The pool is dug out of the Wealden clay by hand, and lined with cement. Then it is filled with water, and as soon as the bottom is covered, we boys are allowed in to swim. The problem is that I still can't swim, even at eleven years old. "Come on" says Peter Lall - my erstwhile enemy - "it's not difficult. You have to get it right in stages. Can you do the 'Dead Man's Float'?" "No. How?" "Well, first you take a deep breath, then you just lie face down on the water with your arms stretched right out above your head. Stay there till your breath runs out. Try it." So I did. "Okay, next you stand against the side of the pool, and as you start the float you kick out against the wall, and see if you can get across." I almost crossed the pool. "This is easy!" "Told you. Now as you go, kick your legs up and down. When your breath runs out, turn your face sideways, and snatch a breath. And keep kicking." I crossed the width twice. "What about arms?" "Now when you breathe, keep your face up, pull your arms down and pretend you are crawling like a baby." Before the pool has even filled, I can swim anywhere by dog paddling. "Alright", says Peter, "you can swim, but it doesn't look good yet. Next you have to reach forward with your arms as far as you can, then pull each one down right under you in turn. Pull each arm up elbow first. Then do it again." By the end of the week, I can do the crawl. And the pool is turning a soupy green colour. Nobody at Tavistock knows about filtering the pool water!

Cow Parsley

Ted Jarvis, the groundsman, is clearing away the laurels and rhododendrons that used to encircle the swimming pool. He is very strong; his bare arms are solid muscle as he chops away with his billhook. But there is a livid blue and yellow bruise on his fore-arm. "How d'you do that, Ted?" "Snakebite. I took hold of a branch last week, and got a handful of adder as well!" I am horrified. All Sussex children know that adders are dangerous, even deadly. "Gosh; didn't it hurt?" "Well, the first one did. But it happens once or twice a year on this job, and now it's only annoying." In the early summer, down by the streams, sometimes the air has an acrid smell that snakes make when they are shedding their skins. Often we see the skins, and sometimes we see snakes. Mostly though they are grass snakes. These can be quite big, four or five foot long. People say grass snakes are harmless. But every time I see one I feel an instinctive thrill of fright, before I get control of it.

The Police

Dad knows to an egg exactly how many chicks will be hatched in the big incubators. The whole setting and incubation process is timed so that the baby chicks hatch the night before market day; their shells crack open, and in the morning there they are, cheeping and staggering a little on the wire grill tray. We pack them up carefully in cardboard boxes, with a little hay to make them comfy. We write whether they are Sussex Whites or Rhode Island Reds on the box. And Dad takes them to the market, where they are sold to other farmers by Percy Watson, the pattering auctioneer. And it is only a matter of counting to be sure that twenty or so are missing from a hatch of five hundred. After months of this, Dad says, "This is worse than taxes. At least you know where taxes are going. Somebody is living off us." In the circumstances Dad thinks it is no use talking to the village Policeman. So he goes to Uckfield, some miles away, and discusses the problem with the CID.

Next hatching night, two detectives and my father are hiding in the oast-house loft. At about two o'clock in the morning, footsteps of two people are heard on the road outside. In the faint moonlight by the gate stands a solid figure holding a bike. A second tall person slips through the gate, crosses the yard, and the door below opens quietly. The police jump down through a trap door: there is a gasp and a curse, then the sound of steps running through the building to the foodstore, and out the back door into the fields. The figure at the gate has vanished. Sherry and Simon are both in the foodstore; and they set off in hot pursuit . Their angry barking fades away up the fields, and over the hill towards the village. A long time later the dogs come back, still very agitated. Sherry has a piece of dirty tweed material in her teeth. It is the only evidence gained from the night's work. The CID watch for two more weeks; but there are no more nocturnal visitors. Now the oast and the hatchery are carefully locked every evening. The losses drop for a while.

Some weeks later Dad says to my Mother "I was in the hairdressers this morning in Heathfield. You know how it is - I suddenly had this spooky feeling that I was being watched. I looked up at the mirror, and I saw a look of pure hatred - to make your blood run cold. It was veiled immediately, but for a moment there was no doubt. Bumper was sitting there, waiting for his turn. He asked politely after everyone's health as I left the shop."

Fire Again

It is sometime during the summer term. I am getting up one morning, and look outside. There is a faint smell of smoke in the air. Then I notice: the brooder house - isn't there! Gone - vanished: I can see straight through to the Possingworth woods! A few bricks remain of the foundations. Dad goes out to look; then he comes back, and I hear him say something to Mother in the kitchen. After a while he goes to the lavatory, which is next to my bedroom. And I hardly dare to recognise the sound I hear: my father is sobbing.

Several people at Tavistock say "You live down the Waldron Road don't you? Did you see the big fire?" I say "No, but it was one of our poultry houses. No-one saw it happen." Except for half the county. No-one thought to call us. Bumper approaches my father. "I was coming up the road with PC Hill before dawn. We saw lights moving along the back corridor. We supposed it was you, checking on the lamps." Of course. And how did he know there was a back corridor? Of course it is quite normal to be walking around the country roads before dawn. It just depends on what you do for a trade.

Holidays

School ends in the third week of July. Rosemary and Penny are going to Tilsmoor School, at the other end of town from Tavistock. Fortunately the Tavistock swimming pool is kept in operation for the local boys and their families to use during the holidays. So we cycle there most days. It is a precious relief from a scorching summer.

Mrs Mackay lives between our Woodfield and Warren Lane. One blistering day we receive a phone call. "Can you come and collect your dog please?" "Why, what's he doing?" "Well, he's lying in our goldfish pond. And he's too big - there's no room for the goldfish! I have tried to pull him out, but he growls at me." Dad goes and brings a chastised Simon home: we don't want trouble with the neighbours.

Mother has inherited Grandpa Bonfield's car - a little maroon Austin Seven 'Ruby', with a permanent tinkling noise that comes from the starting handle sticking through the bottom of the radiator. She calls it Emma-Jane, and is very fond of it. Mother has booked us a seaside holiday, at Brackelsham Bay, close to

Chichester harbour. She takes us there in the car, and it takes much of the day, as we cannot exceed the 30 mph speed limit by very much even outside towns. The sea is fun, now that I can swim. Sometimes we go exploring around the villages and harbours. There is Bosham village - pronounced Bozzam - where we are intrigued to find a rowing boat on the road by the church. They tell us the sea comes in and covers the road at high tide. On the east side of the harbour we can see anchored yachts at Dell Quay. At Itchenor Ferry we sit outside the Ferryboat Inn and sip cider. At Birdham Pool I am allowed to go exploring: there are lots of yachts moored in this harbour, behind the lock gates. I am fascinated: they look so smart with their bright white paint and brilliant varnish. I stare so hard that a man invites me on board his motor yacht. It is like a small house inside - a vision of darkly glowing wood. It makes a lasting impression on me. Maybe the Navy will be like this?

Chestnuts

Autumn

Over the road from us, my friend Mr Field has sold his farm, Hilden House Farm, to a Mr Oaks. Hillary Oaks is a rather diffident person, tallish but slightly stooped, wearing a small ginger moustache to add character to a rather weak face. He shares the farmhouse with another man we never really met. They have bought a small David Brown caterpillar tractor, and they play with it as if it were a new toy. It seems hopelessly impractical for real work on the farm, as it lurches and leaps over the smallest bumps like a bucking bronco. He is raising chickens called Black Anconas, which rapidly become a problem for Dad. They are one of the few breeds able to really fly, and they fly up into the trees along beside the road at night. In the morning, they often come down into our yard, and proceed to help themselves from our foodstore. Dad has had words with Mr Oakes, but he says that neighbours have to solve their own problems, and just laughs it off.

Mr Oaks is a strange kind of man, but not without friends. Indeed Mrs Baker, from Warren Lane, keeps driving very slowly past our farm and his, apparently looking for him like a mooncalf. We call her 'Lindy Loo', and think she is making a fool of herself.

Some strange disease has afflicted the poultry at Selwyns Farm, which is a smallholding of a few acres down Brown's Lane, next door to Mr Oakes fields.. The farm is owned by Miss Gamman, a competent rather mannish woman and her partner Miss Wacey, who keep chickens, and a few ducks on one of the murkiest ponds in the county. The Ministry of Agriculture put up No Entry signs across the gates, and laid disinfectant soaked straw in front of them. Some weeks later we hear that all the poultry had been slaughtered and incinerated; and that she had been compensated for their value. It was the first case of Fowl Pest in Sussex since before the war; the vets thought it must have been brought by a wild bird from France. The incident is a nine-day wonder: but then it passed into local history.

The Fergie

For us, though, things seem to be going quite well. New equipment appears around the house. Dad decides to get a new Morris van for the farm, and it is made up as a shooting brake. For short trips up to the village we are even allowed to sit on the tailboard, with our feet dangling over the road. The old Flying Standard, once Dad's pride and joy, is sold off. The Ute runs on less than half the petrol anyway. Then, completely unannounced, one day when I come home from school there is a new Ferguson tractor standing in the yard. It is a lovely bit of engineering; most of its equipment is carried on a hydraulic lift behind the driver's seat, and bit by bit I find out how the controls work. The first time Dad lets me drive it, I take my foot off the clutch much too fast, and the tractor leaps forward and runs over a wooden chicken-crate. Fortunately it was empty! Dad bites his lip, and says "Next time, lift your foot slowly" And like many farmer's sons, I am soon allowed to drive the tractor anywhere on the farm, though not on the roads.

At Christmas time Dad says "Its been a long time since we had a real treat. How about the Circus?" We are all delighted. We pile into the Ute, and Dad drives us up to London. We have ringside seats at the Olympia circus. We get sprayed with foam by the clowns; we gasp at the lions and tigers, and we giggle at the elephants holding each others tails. Rosemary, who kept up riding when I abandoned it, is enchanted by the horses with their flowing manes and sparkling bridles, and envious of the long-legged girls who ride them standing on their backs. Penny and Patrick just look on in starry-eyed amazement. When it is all over, Dad takes us to The Victoria Hotel, beside the railway station, " For a good supper". "I have never tasted turbot" he says; "let's try it". A wine bucket appears, and eventually a huge flat fish on a wide dish is placed before us, and solemnly filleted by the head waiter. He is wearing a long tail-coat and a black bow tie. I have never even dreamed of anywhere so smart in all my country life!

If Dad has financial worries, he doesn't discuss them with us. Sometimes Mother lets something slip. But they try to keep us unworried, and by and large they succeed.

Shadow

We are sitting at the kitchen table; Mother is scrambling eggs for breakfast. As she cracks one open, she makes a face, then tips it away into the waste strainer. "That's the second this week with a blood clot in it", she says.

Bryony – Woody Nightshade

1950

A reminder. As explained in the Introduction to this book, I have chosen to tell my father's story in his own voice, and as far as possible in his own words. From here on, the 'I' in the altered font used below is my father, William Armstrong Brown, poultry farmer aged 39 at this point. 'I', his son Robin, am twelve. The story told here separates as far as possible what he - and later we all - knew at the time from what was discovered much later.

My Father's Story†

In November 1949 there was a case of Fowl Pest confirmed at Selwyns Farm in Cross-in-Hand. The stock was slaughtered. The owner Miss Gamman sought to blame the infection on our mutual neighbour Mr Oakes, saying that his birds were flying over amongst hers. The three farms - Selwyns, Hilden House, and the Old Farm, were adjacent to each other, and were spread over a distance of only about 350 yards between the farmhouses. (In fact, the minimum separation between Selwyns Farm and my own was the width of one field - 130 yards.) At that time, Fowl Pest Regulations required all farms within half a mile of an outbreak to be inspected by the Ministry of Agriculture Animal Health Division Veterinary Officers. I believe that the vet concerned did visit Mr Oakes to warn him, but the farm was not inspected; and he never informed me of any danger nor visited my farm. Selwyn was infected, and some 1000 birds at Hilden were alleged to be in contact (via flying Anconas), both with Selwyn and with a further 4000 birds at the Old Farm. In those days almost all poultry were running outdoors: from the point of view of a virus disease it was virtually one farm. A glance at the map will show the appalling risk taken by the Ministry vet in not inspecting the adjacent farms at the time of the infection.

I was certainly free from trouble at this time, but it started soon afterwards. Losses occurred in a rearing field into which Oakes' birds were continually flying. However I had never seen Fowl Pest at the time; indeed very few people had. The information we had was that it was an explosive disease with a very high death rate, and one had to report it at once before all one's stock was gone. It appears that Oakes soon got into trouble and had many losses, presumably not knowing any more than I did what was the cause. He became ill himself too, and the smell of his dead birds when he carried them out of his rearing house was horrible even across the road. Becoming ashamed of them as they looked so ill, he kept them shut in their houses out of sight.

Eventually on Feb 21st someone notified the RSPCA. A man went round Oakes' farm, called in the police, and they found many dead and dying poultry. Oakes was found, I believe a vet was called, specimens were opened of which the crop and gizzard were found to be empty, and they all jumped to the conclusion that the birds were being starved to death. Other suspicious matters were found at the farm too: Oakes was informed that a very serious view was taken of all this, and he could expect a prosecution to follow. At this time the police came to my house to notify Captain Elvin ... then Divisional Vetinary Officer of the Ministry of Agriculture in Lewes, who had taken over from the vet who certified the outbreak at Selwyns Farm. I do not know what part, if any, Captain Elvin played in the case against Oakes. I am told by the RSPCA that it is routine to notify Divisional Officers in these cases of poultry, for the express purpose of eliminating this very risk of confusing disease with maltreatment.

Before the case was heard ... Oakes, very seriously worried, had been to the local police saying it was ridiculous to accuse him of not feeding the birds - they were sick and would not eat, and kept on dying. He asked "What should I do?" The local policeman replied "If they were my birds, I would put them in the market before they all die!" This he did.

However by this time (March 1950) my losses had begun to worry me so much I decided to keep enough of the young stock to make up my laying flock to capacity, and scrap the rest. I put my doubtful stock in the same weekly market. About ten days later another MoA vet, a Mr Hunter, came round and said he wanted to inspect the farm, as the buyer of my birds in the market had got Fowl Pest. I was quite flabbergasted, but admitted that I had experienced some losses from growing stock. He inspected the farm and expressed himself well satisfied with the remaining stock, but warned me to let him know if anything untoward occurred. He then asked where Oakes was living, saying he had sold in the market too. Oakes was out. Hunter returned next Sunday morning: he banged violently on Oakes back door and dragged him out to see the birds: apparently there were many dead and dying again. Mr Hunter appeared to be laying down the law in no uncertain terms. The fact remains that no action was apparently taken to investigate the possibility of disease at Hilden Farm..

The case went forward in May: Oakes pleaded guilty on the advice of another vet, on the grounds that the evidence (of starvation) was overwhelming. A poultryman of my experience would have asserted that the evidence of the crop and gizzard being empty was not even relevant, as sick birds do not eat. Oakes was disgraced in public by this conviction: he later sold Hilden Farm, and left the county. I was not aware of some details given here at the time, having only been told them by Oakes years later.

Economics

The new brooder house is nearly finished. It is very different from the old one. It is almost twice as big, with brick walls, and it has a concrete base and an asbestos roof, with asbestos internal walls for the pens. The heating comes from radiators under the platforms in each pen, and they in turn are heated by a big coke-fired boiler outside the building. It is all as near fireproof as can be. And it will be much more economical too, as coke is much cheaper than paraffin. Dad had some builders in to do the walls and foundations; but he has done all the roofing and piping himself. I am helping with the last sections of the roof and the gutters. Then I paint the sliding doors and the window shutters with creosote.

The government controls are forcing down the price paid for milk to the point where a dairy farm of twenty six acres cannot really make a living. Dad slowly reduces the number of cows, to reduce the amount of work on the endless milking. Over the course of the year he builds up the stock of breeding poultry to supply more fertile eggs to fill the incubators, and thus to breed more chickens from the brooder house. Mr Duprey is a good friend of my father. He has a real financial problem. He lives on Newpond Hill over towards Little London, near where the Messerschmidt crashed, and he has only nine acres. He also has six children, of about our ages. They also have decided that the only answer is to farm intensively; concentrate on poultry for meat, and to reduce their dairy herd. Mrs Duprey also runs a riding stable at the farm. I tried riding there once, when I was six. The donkey ran away with me, and brushed me off under a tree branch. I didn't repeat the experiment! The Dupreys are Belgian, though they came to England before the war. They still speak French among themselves. Mrs Duprey is a born organiser. The Village Show was her idea; and she is always organising coach trips to the seaside, or to pantomimes in Brighton. Where she leads, plenty of people will follow.

> In May I had to go into hospital for a minor operation. I left instructions for the remaining young stock to be moved to the breeding pens. Within a few days what appeared to be 'colds' appeared among the adjacent older birds. While I was in hospital these rapidly got worse, the egg production collapsed and many of the older birds died. I could not find the name of the MoA vet who called before, so I called in the Poultry Advisory Officer: he opined that some of the young chicks had coccidiosis (a common inflammation of the gut), which is never a problem with older birds.

Cricket

My father has found an outlet for his favourite sport - cricket. He had been a good all-round cricketer in his youth, and had even captained the fathers team at a Tavistock Sports Day. Now he has joined the Waldron village team, and is playing regularly on Saturdays at home in the village, and travelling around the county too. I watch them, and sometimes travel with the team to away matches at other villages. My father seems to become a different person away from the farm. The tiredness falls way, he plays well, and is full of jokes and good humour. For an afternoon each week, he becomes a different man. A much happier man. He is a reliable batsman, a good slow spin bowler, and a good catch. It is not long before he is made team captain by the Waldron Cricket Club.

Bill Smith, the landlord of the Star Inn opposite the church in Waldron, has a huge old pre-war Austin A16, which is big enough at a pinch to take almost the whole eleven. I watch them setting off, with the old engine chuffing quietly, more like a steam engine than a petrol driven one. It is the high point of the week for all of them. Our dog Simon, who always goes with my father, becomes the team mascot. So at home matches, particularly after a win, they all adjourn to the Star afterwards, for a glass or two. And usually they put a half pint on the floor for Simon. And this season there are lots of wins. The villages of East Sussex have an Evening Cricket League, where they compete on a midweek evening for the

Oakshot Cup. It is a straight knockout competition; and it is cricket unlike any other known sort of this noble but rather boring game. Each side has twenty overs only. So it is big hitters against the fastest bowlers for both sides. A side is seldom all-out, but there is no bonus in playing for time as draws are not allowed - you either win or you lose. Really exciting stuff. And as the season goes on they are still in the Cup. I watch the final match, which is at Old Heathfield. Bill Kemp, the thundering fast bowler and a very powerful batsman, is probably the hero of the match, but we also have plenty of others, Bill Smith, Ken Hook, and Ray Petit the wicket keeper. And we won in the last over of the game, with only three more balls to play in the fading evening light! My father steps forward in front of the team to receive the cup from the Oakshots, the Squire of Foxhunt Manor and his wife. Our whole family are there, watching and cheering. I am excited, and hugely proud of my father.

Scouts

The 2nd Heathfield Troop, Tavistock Hall. So say our shoulder badges. Two years ago our PT teacher offered to form a Scout Troop, and a Wolf Cub pack for the younger boys. Percy F. Wyman is a walking tribute to physical and moral clean living, having survived three days of lying injured and left for dead on the battlefield of the Somme in the First World War. He says he was 'sent back'. Our small Scout troop has two patrols, the Swifts and the Kestrels. I rise to be Second of the Kestrels. We play tracking games, leaving secret signs, along the paths and trails all through Tavistock woods. We learn how to light fires with only two matches, and we try unsuccessfully to set light to wood shavings with a little bow and a pointed stick. We learn to do semaphore with flags, and try to learn Morse code with hand torches. This goes on for a couple of years. Mr Wyman is promoted to District Scoutmaster, next in rank below the District Commissioner. He organises another camp, this time a Scout camp, on our old campground at Magham Down.

Mr Wyman arrives at the campsite in great concern. "Whatever is the matter?" he asks; "what has gone wrong? I came as soon as I got your message!" "Nothing is the matter" we said. "Then why are you flying a distress signal?" The only flag flying is the Union Jack, which I hoisted that morning. Looking more closely, I see that it is upside down. Oh, the shame!

This is the last time I see many of the boys who have been there throughout my schooldays. Michael Oakley, a natural clown, and son of the owner of the Burwash garage; and Robert Banks his best friend, the very nicely brought-up son of a Burwash farmer are leaving. John Mannock, a pleasant chap and head boy is leaving, as are Kim Gordon and Alan Rathbone, two rumbustuous spirits; and Bob Castledene is even going to Eastbourne College - my destination. Only Andrew and I remain of the sixth form, and other boys move up from the fifth. Our classes for my last year at Tavistock become almost private tutorials with Mrs Ward.

In the summer of 1950 I experienced very heavy losses. I tried all the treatments I knew for 'colds', and sent birds to laboratories for post mortem examinations. Some of the results - bloody mucous and brain inflammation - should have warned the lab experts , and me also (had I known then what I came to know later) of the obvious suggestion of the presence of fowl pest. But the blame was put on the design of the new brooder house, which was suspected of producing down-draughts and chilling the very young chicks, setting off the respiratory problems which were the root of all the trouble. In the autumn rearing was stopped for a time, to test for draughts and make modifications. The chicken houses were sterilised.

During this time of rationing demand and prices for poultry were high, and I was able to survive through commercial sales of eggs and dead poultry. Sales of live birds were stopped, as I was a fairly well known and successful breeder, and anxious to preserve my reputation.

The severe losses from the poultry stock throughout the whole year, added to the loss of production the previous year from the brooder house destruction, pushed the farm into severe financial difficulties. Stock that die have had to be fed all their lives, and there is no economic return on this investment of both money and time. I was forced to raise funds from my relatives in order to re-stock the farm.

1951

Robin Ploughing

"In Sickness and in Health"

Since her big operation, my mother is not the woman she was. She mixes mash for the breeding hens by hand, as she cannot start the Lister. Then, with each of us carrying as much as we can manage in sacks on our backs, we set off round the henhouses. It is January, and our boots break through the frozen crust on the mud, up nearly to our knees. Dad is in bed with a violent septic throat. This frequently happens in winter; he has a weak throat. Once, early in the war, he was sent to Tunbridge Wells Hospital. He heard later, by a round-about route, that his throat was so bad they thought he was a failed suicide - from swallowing acid! Suicide is shameful: nursing suicides is distasteful, sympathy would be misplaced. They treated him very coldly, and he discharged himself before he was better. The men run the farm during the week, with us lending a hand. At the weekends Mother and we kids have to do it all ourselves. Rosemary and Penny handle the egg collections.

Quinzy is the old name for a suppurating throat infection. Before the war it was frequently fatal, but now bitter M&B drugs and penicillin can get control of it. Even so, it takes three weeks for Dad to get fit. Dr Cuddiford takes some swabs from his throat, and comes to a nasty conclusion. "You have been drinking some very dirty water. Do you ever drink from a ditch?" "Just occasionally, I dip a handful when I am thirsty". "Well, I advise you not to. And check where that ditch comes from." The ditch that runs down from the top of the farm was thought to come from a spring on Highlands Farm next door. Dad goes over to have a look, and finds not a spring, but a medium size pond surrounded by dense gorse bushes, with heavy wheel tracks leading to it. And suddenly he realises that this is where the Durrants pump out the cess-wagons!

Churchill.

I am sitting in the Plaza cinema in Heathfield. After the newsreel, with its quacky announcers who sound like Army officers, there is a special film. Winston Churchill, our great wartime leader, is sitting in an armchair holding his trademark cigar. "The British people have had their fill of Socialism, of controls, of rationing, inspectors, informers, and all the apparatus of a bureaucratic state. It is not our way. In the coming election, if you will vote Conservative, we will abolish all of this bureaucratic control of our lives. Leaving only the proper organs of government, we will burn all of the red tape and set the people free!" It is a heady message, though it does not please everyone in the audience: some cheer and some grumble aloud.

We take the election propaganda into school, and plaster the little sixth form room with notices from both sides. Andrew's parents are socialists, and of course so is he. I am puzzled about this, as they are comfortably-off professional people. Doctor Soddy is in fact a psychiatrist, and his great-uncle was a famous scientist. I can understand poor people wanting to work less and take some of the rich people's money; but why should the better-off people want that? Social justice is not in my agenda. Our debates over who was to blame for the depression - before either of us were born - have all the passion we have inherited from our families. It is not a good recipe for friendship. I take the arguments home, to the meal table. Eventually my father bursts out "Oh, for heavens sake shut up! You don't understand anything!" I am mortified: it is the only time he has ever spoken to me like that. And I thought he agreed too; after all, he is the source of most of my strident political opinions.

But the Conservatives win the election by a slender three seats; and they keep their main promise. Within a year rationing has gone. Almost the last goods to be de-rationed are sweets.

Re-start

In the spring of 1951 a fresh start was made, and for a
time things were a little better: although the growth of

the young birds was poor, at least the mortality was low. Then, during a few hot days in June, the trouble flared up again and ran through the whole brooder house of 3000 chicks, causing heavy losses reminiscent of the previous year. Mortality in some sections was above 60%; the older stock outside showed every sign of the same disease. I saw an article in a poultry magazine about a variant form of fowl pest, which was called the sub-acute type, and which described many of the symptoms seen on the farm for more than a year. I called in the Ministry vets again.

Mr Burns came from Lewes. He was non-committal about the chicks and the adult birds. I was renting a field on Mr McCreadie's nearby farm for raising growing stock in folds. When Mr Burns saw these he became very serious, and said were it not for the large number of birds involved (6000) he would certify fowl pest on the spot. As it was, he felt he should take some tests and make some other enquiries. He carried out some post mortem examinations on young chicks, and went out of his way to point out many symptoms to myself and my wife. He showed us how to mark the records, saying all losses from this day would be compensated, and placed the farm under a standstill order, saying that in a few days they would come in and clean us up.

He returned a few days later and took some blood samples. It was then he began questioning me on the origin of the disease. When did I first have trouble? Had I bought any stock from markets or other sources? It appeared the Ministry couldn't understand the source of the infection, as the county had been free for some months. Thinking I had nothing to hide I told him quite honestly that, if this was fowl pest, I had had it for months, and traced it to when I had last imported birds in the spring of 1950. (This of course was the date of the trouble with Oakes' birds.) However I did not mention his name, having by then completely forgotten about him. On either the first or the second visit Burns remarked to one of my employees that, while on many investigations of fowl pest there were doubts at first, in this case there was no doubt at all.

When he returned next time his manner had entirely changed. He became very brusque and said he would have to take more blood tests; implying, though he did not say, that there had been no reaction from the previous tests. He began to play down the possibility of fowl pest, although he offered no alternative. "Have you had losses in the Incubators?" I said "No, although the fertility has been dreadfully bad." He seemed to seize on that. "Ah well, if it had really been fowl pest - and I did think it might be when I first came - you would certainly have had losses in the incubator itself." I had no idea of this. Burns left hurriedly. I felt I was left facing absolute ruin. I had not been able to beat this trouble, in spite of months of trying everything I had ever heard of.

A few days later a hatch was due out of the incubator. The previous night I had noticed that it looked quite good. Most of the chicks were almost dry, and ready to be taken out. On going next morning to pack the chicks, I found more than half were not only dead but already decomposed, and stinking horribly. Remembering what Burns had told me, I phoned the MoA Lewes office and asked to speak to him: I told him what had happened, and asked him to re-open the case. He refused quite bluntly to return to the farm, saying "There is nothing I can do for you". The next week the same thing recurred. Desperate, I again phoned the Animal Health Department in Lewes. This time, the call having been anticipated, the girl who answered said as soon as I gave my name "You are not to phone this office worrying us. We only deal with notifiable diseases". Here I was, reporting every symptom of a notifiable disease, and the office created for the purpose refused even to answer the phone! Officially, the farm did not have fowl pest. When the Advisory Officer repeated his ludicrous advice about coccidiosis, I asked the advisor of a well known animal food company. He was appalled. He said "Your only hope is to treat the condition as if it were legally fowl pest. You have to kill out all the stock, and leave the farm depopulated for a time so that the virus has no host, then you clean up thoroughly and restock". I sold about 1000 of the least affected birds as meat at Smithfield market. But of the 6000 I had when Burns was first called in, 5000 died, or were culled and incinerated.

The Exam

"Do well - it matters". Those are my mother's parting words as I leave to take the Eastbourne Scholarship exam. I go down to Eastbourne by bus, and find my way to the College at the appointed hour. There are six of us who are staying for the three days of the exams. We have our meals in Blackwater House, on the end of one of the long tables in the dining room; and we are the objects of mild curiosity from the boarders there. Bob Castledene, who left Tavistock last year, seeks me out. "Its not too bad here. But don't go to School House; they are all bullies, and the new boys have a miserable time." Blackwater is a tall rather sinister looking redbrick building, something like a cross between Lewes Gaol and the entrance to Auschweiz. There are exams all day for three days on all the Common Entrance subjects. But these exams are harder. There are about twenty candidates in all. We six sleep at the Sanitorium, which is empty as no-one is ill. It is a light and sunny place. But sleeping is difficult, as the huge bell of the Town Hall clock chimes away the hours all night. You can hear it all over the town, and the College houses are not more than a quarter of a mile away.

When the results arrive, I have gained admission, but I have not won a scholarship. Mrs Ward is annoyed with me. "You should have done better. You are not stupid." Mother says sadly, "A scholarship would really have helped." My father says nothing. Then I hear that the plans to send Rosemary to Ashford School for Girls are dropped. She had been looking forward to it. But the farm cannot pay two sets of secondary school fees. I feel bad about it, but it's too late now. Rosemary takes the 'eleven-plus' exam for Lewes Grammar School, and passes very well from Tilsmoor. This is a considerable success, as East Sussex only lets one child in ten go to Grammar School. At her final Tilsmoor Sports Day, she falls heavily early in the senior girls hurdles, but grits her teeth and carries on with long jumps and high jumps. Next day, the doctor diagnoses a broken wrist. Penny, just coming up for her eighth birthday, enjoys herself in the speciality races like the three-legged race and the egg-and-spoon race. Patrick watches solemnly; in the autumn next year he will be starting school too.

A Day at the Races

Auntie Yoe and her new husband Jack Carnaghan arrive, together with his brother Don and some other people in two cars. They have called in on the way to the Races at Plumpton, along from Lewes under the shadow of the Downs. I am invited to go along with them for the day. I take along some pocket money for lunch. When we get there, they have brought a big picnic. Uncle Jack, a tall plausible Irishman, but very friendly in an absent-minded way, explains the system of betting. "You choose your horse, either because you believe the tipsters or because you like the look of him, then you look for which bookie is giving the longest odds on him winning. Don't take too long, as the odds are changing all the time. Then you place your bet, and he gives you a scribbled ticket with the horse's number, your odds, and the amount you bet. If you lose, you've lost it. If you win, he gives you your bet times the odds, and he returns your stake money too". So I go to the paddock, and look for tall horses with slender but strong hocks, and I place a few bets. I won something on three, and lost on two others in eight races. At the end of a long day I am over a pound ahead. The five grown-ups in the party have all lost money! I sit in the car all the way home feeling quietly pleased at my judgement.

The Ploughboy

Dad says, "Since you love driving the tractor, I am going to teach you something really useful". And he teaches me to plough. You have to lay out the field so that you plough across the slope, never up-and-down, to prevent rainwater washing the soil away. You plough a straight line of furrows one way, then you return in the other direction about twenty yards away, with the tops of the furrows facing outwards. When the two sets meet, you start another pattern. You do not plough right to the edge of the field, but leave a space called a headland for turning the tractor and plough around. When all except the headlands are ploughed, you start at the inner edge of the headland, and plough round the whole field several times until you reach the outside. Ploughmen are very proud of their neat and even work on a field, and the straightness of their furrows. I work all day on a rented field, down along the Under-Road. I think I am as happy as I have ever been, driving the tractor here in the sunshine. At the top of my young voice I am singing the Scarecrow's Song, which my mother taught me.

> *I once was an elegant fellow, dainty and dapper and gay;*
> *With a coat of most beautiful yellow, which I wore in a beautiful way.*
> *And though now in sunshine and rain I stand,*
> *In sunshine and fast falling rain;*
> *No matter whatever befalls me, I always will sing this refrain—*
> *Fol de rol, fol de rol, fol de rol-ay,*
> *I scare away crows the whole of the day.*
> *I clap my clappers, and flourish my flappers,*
> > *Away!   Away!   Away!*

At sunset I drive the tractor home, well pleased with my day's work. I would have asked my father's permission to drive on the road; and he would have said no, as I am too young and don't have a license. But he isn't here to ask. It is the last day of my childhood.

Alfriston Down from Litlington

Part 2

Son of the Downs

We have no waters to delight
Our broad and brookless vales –
Only the dewpond on the height
Unfed, that never fails –
Whereby no tattered herbage tells
Which way the season flies –
Only our close-bit thyme that smells
Like dawn in Paradise.

Here through the strong and shadeless days
The tinkling silence thrills;
Or little, lost, Down churches praise
The Lord who made the hills:
But here the Old Gods guard their round,
And, in her secret heart,
The heathen kingdom Wilfred found
Dreams, as she dwells, apart.

Sussex. Rudyard Kipling.

Going Away

Mother took me to Brighton during the holidays, to buy me the clothes that are required to be a College Boy. I was fitted up with long trousers to replace my shorts, and a new grey tweed sports jacket. Then there was a dark blue suit, and two Van Heusen shirts with detachable collars, and a set of collar studs to hold them in place. The list said I needed several changes of vests and pants, and she ordered a reel of name tapes so that everything would come back to me. I needed rugby kit, and new boots, and a multitude of other equipment. I was embarrassed about the cost of it all, it seemed horribly extravagant for a farm boy.

We loaded my trunk into the back of the Ute. Mother gave me a parting hug, and said "Remember this. My Grandfather once said to me - "Whatever thy hand findest to do - do thy damnedest!" " Nonie grinned, and simply said "Good luck Bobby". As we turned onto the concrete new road by Hailsham, Dad squeezed my knee and said "Are you worried Charles?" It is my second name, but no-one ever uses it, and for a moment I wondered who he was talking to. No, I was not worried really; just a bit nervous about being dumped into a whole new life this afternoon. I had been Head Boy at Tavistock, less by talent than by the fact that almost everyone older than me had left. I wasn't particularly proud of it: when my parents asked last spring "Who is Head Boy this year?", I replied "I suppose I am." It hadn't seemed worth a special announcement. But if I could manage that, I hoped I was up whatever was waiting for me.

We drove over Willingdon hill, with the Long Man of Wilmington looking blankly down on us, then down the other side into Eastbourne itself. Dad pulled up at a tall brick building with grey chipped-flint facings, and we got out. My father had been an Eastbourne College boy himself in Crosby House. Years ago Crosby had been amalgamated with Wargrave House, and the two buildings were now joined by a bridge at the first floor level. Between us we carried the trunk up four flights of stairs to my dormitory on the top floor. Mr Rodd, the new housemaster, showed Dad around for a while, and left me to get acquainted with Tom Kammerling, a solitary new boy like myself, in Prep Room North - which was to be my home for a year. One by one, my new schoolmates assembled. Then a hand-bell clanged through the building, and we all trooped across the bridge to the dining room for supper. We sat at two long tables, with fifteen a side. Big tureens of baked beans and sausages were passed along the table with fried bread; seniors first, then juniors, and we all served ourselves. It wasn't haute cuisine, but it was a lot better than Tavistock!

The prefects called all the new boys to their study, and Gordon Crumley the head of the house welcomed us. He said "I expect most of you have read Tom Brown's School Days?" We had. "Well, Eastbourne, and particularly Wargrave, is not like that. We will not tolerate bullies or bullying. We want you to be happy here, as this will be your home for most of the year. On the other hand, you have come to a very competitive school; and we expect you to work very hard in class, and to play very hard in sports. There is no place here for slackers of any sort. We have a cadet corps here. It is voluntary, but everyone in the school is in it: you would be very well advised to join too. Choose your friends from among yourselves: we do not encourage mixing between years, or with other houses. For the next two weeks you will have to learn an awful lot about the College. You will each have a guide, who is charged with teaching you all the school rules, and showing you all your classrooms, and the limits of bounds. And you will have to learn how to recognise all the special insignia - ties caps and badges, by which the College rewards those who succeed. In two weeks we will give you a test on all this. If you fail, your guide will be in trouble! So do not let him down. After that, for the rest of this year you will do fagging about once a week. This is not terrible at all. In Wargrave it simply means that you get the prefects afternoon tea, and polish their shoes if they ask you. It is a public school tradition: you must learn to serve, before you can expect to be served in your turn. If you respect the rules you should not have any trouble here. If you break the rules, you will find out that we will be severe with anyone who lets us down. But if you do have troubles, see us. We are your family, and we look after our own. Now go to bed, and sleep well. A new life begins in the morning." The huge bell of the Town Hall clock clanged all the quarters until ten thirty, and then the hours all night long. It quickly became the measure of my life.

Academe

I found I was assigned to the first year: as far as I knew, all the other scholarship candidates went straight into the second year. I must have done pretty badly on the exam! The trouble was that the first year classes simply went back to repeat the last year's work at prep school, or even further. I had wanted to get on with some proper science, but I only got biology. Before half term I was thoroughly bored. The only redeeming feature was that I got art and metalwork classes, with both of them taught simply as techniques like recipes - "do this, and you will see that it works". The only drawing techniques I know now are those I learned in just one term. Mr Simpson, then and since, was rated as a brilliant teacher.

Eastbourne College

After a few nervous days of finding my classrooms, life settled into a pretty exhausting routine. The day started with bells at seven fifteen, and again at seven thirty, for waking up and getting dressed. Anyone missing the third bell was likely to find no breakfast. We then prepared our books, and walked down to chapel for a brief hymn-and-a-prayer daily service before the first two classes. The masters waited outside the classroom for a customary two minutes. When they entered, always wearing a working black academic robe, there was perfect silence. Everyone stood up: it was a ritual mark of respect. Anyone turning up after the master was already in trouble. "Please sit down." In the first class of the day, we made a gesture at bible study of the text of the morning lesson in chapel. Eastbourne College after all is an Anglican school. The masters mostly asked one member of the class to read the lesson again, aloud. Then "Any questions?": by tacit agreement of boys and teachers alike, there were never any questions. "Alright then. Where did we get to last time?" And the day was off and running.

We had PT in the mid-morning break. We divided up into groups of a dozen or so, and did simple physical jerks, with a lot of team games of tag and similar un-serious stuff. It was administered by senior boys; while it probably got the circulation going, we mostly regarded it as a genial waste of time. As soon as the whistle shrilled, we pulled off our white sweaters and dashed to the Tuck Shop, hoping to get one of the limited supply of hot sausage rolls. Then it was back into class for two more lessons before lunch.

The Eighth Game, and Other Diversions

For sports we went through a rapid sifting process: first into those who had played rugby before and those who hadn't. I hadn't. We had a five minutes explanation of the rules, and were divided into two teams; then we were turned loose on each other. After twenty minutes there was another sifting into ones who showed promise, and the rest. I joined the rest. The College was divided from top to bottom into odd and even games, each of thirty boys. In each year the first third fifth and seventh games were selected for the teams that represented the school in each age group. The even games simply played for exercise and no glory. I quickly found that, although I tried very hard, I simply could not face a frontal tackle: I dived at someone's knees, but I always missed. My instinctive reactions, after the cricket ball in the mouth, simply took me out of the way of anything coming fast at my head. As far as the College could see, or cared to know, I was gutless, and therefore I was classed as a 'weed'. But although I was small for my age, I could run quite fast, so I got a regular position as a fly half in the even games. Expectations were not too high, and rugger on those terms was quite good fun. But I quickly realised that, for the boys and for most of the masters, prowess at rugger or cricket was the only thing that really counted in school society. There were about forty different ties and badges for school colours in major and minor sports, and only one insignificant tie for those who rose to the sixth form for academic aptitude (or simple survival!). Few people even bothered to buy it.

The College was short of playing fields; there were not enough for all four hundred boys to play simultaneously. So in the short winter days we could not have games every day. However some exercise every day was obligatory; quite what you did was a choice of your house. In Wargrave the minimum bid was the Paradise run. This went uphill to a pretty road called Paradise Drive, which looped under the woods and above the Royal Eastbourne Golf Links, then turned downhill to Summerdown playing fields, back past the Memorial athletics course and the Sussex County Cricket Ground, and so to Blackwater Road and home. In my first year this took me nearly fifteen minutes: I managed to knock about a minute a year off this time. Or, if you were training for something special, there was The Horseshoe run. This was a much tougher affair, as you had to run up above the village of Meads to the top of the Downs, then through the thorn bushes across the top of a dry valley, then down the other side past Paradise Wood, and so home. This took anything up to thirty minutes, and left you feeling wrung out. Still, after a necessary shower, the rest of the afternoon was your own, till evening classes started again at a quarter to five.

Compared to many public schools, the College was generous with free time and 'Bounds'. We were allowed to wander freely in all the areas between Terminus Road and the Downs, avoiding only the less choice sectors between the station and Pevensey marshes. In town we had to wear our school caps: in the countryside even that requirement was quite flexible. On Sunday afternoons we were locked outside from two till four pm, unless the weather was atrocious. So we went down to the bandstand on the seafront, hoping to see the girls of Beresford or Moira House schools. Of course, they were forbidden to talk to us, or even to look at us! Or we walked up to the Downs, to the top of Beachy Head, or even back along the ridge towards Wilmington. From up there I could pick out the Fir Grove at the top of the farm on the skyline: it was strangely comforting to see it from my new and rather hard world.

Christmas Holidays

Back home again, in a place so totally familiar, I felt at first like a visitor from another planet. Boarding schools set out to be your total environment, and they succeed to the point of making your own home feel like a foreign country at first. But it soon wore off: families and farm life soon knock off any aloofness. Even so, all boarding school children have to learn to handle two totally different ways of living, and somehow learn not to upset the denizens of either world. It was good to be home.

Penny told me "Simon missed you terribly for weeks. He sat in Daddy's chair sulking all day. He was watching for you through the window, and he pressed his nose against it so hard that he pushed out the little pane in the corner!"

Nonie had slowly made herself accepted at Lewes Grammar School, and seemed to be doing well there. When she started at Lewes she met a lot of prejudice, not only among the girls but also the staff, as she was the only girl in the year to have come from a prep-school and not from a village school. Class prejudice is a two-way street.

On the farm the poultry meat trade appeared to be flourishing. Dad had raised several hundred chicken for the Christmas trade, using old-fashioned feeding techniques he had learned from the Sussex fatteners before the war. The Ministry of Agriculture experts advise filling feeders with dry mash every few days; fed this way the chickens just peck desultorily at the food now and again, and have to take frequent sips of water to swallow the dry powder. Fed at mealtimes with wet mash, they are clamouring for food, and swallow the lot, leaving the trough empty. It is more work, but it is easy to see which technique will fatten chickens more quickly. Because dry mash is disagreeable, the commercial feed compounders use very high protein grains to get the chickens to gain weight. Of course the compounders consult with the experts and the Ministry of Agriculture vets, to persuade them to push their products. Dad ignores the 'expert' advice, and blends his own feed using local grains, saving money too. So we had a prosperous Christmas.

But at Christmas lunch, after a delicious first course of turkey with all the trimmings, Mother watched anxiously as we tucked into the Christmas pudding. "Is it alright?" she asked. "Of course, it's lovely as always." She breathed a sigh of relief. "You see, I had mixed the pudding, and I was just adding the sugar and spice, when I saw from the labels that I had mistaken the allspice, and poured in cayenne pepper instead! I had to throw away the mixture. But I couldn't replace all the dried fruit and raisins from South Africa - I had been saving them for months! So I washed the mixture with a lot of water and the fruit floated, so I saved it with a sieve and used it again!" Some luxuries, like sugar and dried fruit, were still rationed.

1952

Promotion

Back again at Wargrave House I found a little note pinned to my prep-room desk. "See Me" T.E.R. Oh no! Only back in the door by seconds, and already in trouble? "You wanted to see me Sir?" "Ah yes, Brown. Come in. I thought I had better warn you in advance. You are promoted to the Second Year. So you should go down to the Main Building now to work out your new timetable for tomorrow morning. These are your sets for the Second Year". He handed me a list. "And a word of warning. You will be working more at your level; but the classes you are joining have already been working on the O-Level syllabus for three months. You will have to borrow their classroom notes and make your own. You will have only four and a half terms work before you take O-Levels. We are trusting that you won't disappoint us. Good luck!" Once outside I studied the list. I was in the B sets for Physics and Chemistry and most of the other subjects, except C for Latin and French. This was more like it! I looked again at the list: art and metalwork were not mentioned. A pity, but I could live with that. I found that two other boys were promoted with me, out of an intake of a hundred.

The Choir

After my first term in the congregation, which had 'congregational practice' every Friday morning during break, I began to notice that the sound the choir made was, in some mysterious way, better. So I asked for an audition; and I was accepted, at the age of fourteen, still as a treble. Next morning I took my new place somewhere in the front row, opened my hymnbook with its confusing harmony notation, and opened my mouth to sing. And froze. All around me, surrounding me and swallowing me up, the music was moving in all directions. Nearly sixty voices singing four different melodies, moving and blending with each other and with that unforgettable pipe-organ opposite, were playing a musical chess game of notes to make the morning hymn. I knew about tunes - this was something else entirely, something I had not dreamed even existed. I was literally sensually overwhelmed - drowning in the music of living harmony. The College has always been proud of its choir, and the impact it made on me that morning is with me still. It was a gift for life. It was three days before I recovered enough to actually open my mouth and join in.

My room-mates were unimpressed. "Oh Nyaaar - RC reckons he can sing! Don't get above yourself now". In a boarding school there is a continual pressure coming from nearly all the other pupils: no-one must stand-out - except of course at sport. The nail which sticks up will be beaten down. If the older boys deigned to notice the younger ones at all, it was in the expectation of respect or obedience. Competition at all levels was encouraged, and even enforced in sports. In academic work boys were sorted into 'sets' from A to D according to their abilities in different subjects, so everyone could work more or less at their own level. But within those sets the work was marked quite severely. So there was pressure from most of the masters to keep trying hard. This was reinforced by the visits to the Headmaster. For those who got two or more A's in a fortnight this was brief and cordial. For those who got even one D, (not trying), or too many C's, the experience was much less pleasant. The whole school, including the masters, were very much in awe of the Headmaster Mr Nugee, known to us as The Head Man, or simply The Man. His word was law to the whole school.

It is perhaps worth explaining how 'public schools' got their name. In contrast to the free state schools which are open to all members of the public, the 'public schools' have to be paid for, and the fees are expensive. One has to go back more than a century to see where the confusion arose, before universal state education came in about 1870. Before then the two options were private education at home by a tutor; or alternatively education at schools which had more teachers, and were open to pupils recruited from the public at large, and hence called Public Schools. A few have been going for centuries, and have long traditions. Many more were founded in the nineteenth century to educate the children of the growing middle classes. All schools, from the big public schools to the town grammar schools to the village Dame Schools, had to be funded somehow. These fees fell on parents or relatives of the pupils, unless they were lucky enough to obtain scholarships, or places at schools run by guilds or charitable foundations.

Eastbourne,
The Beginning of the Cliffs

Disarmament

Like many schoolboys we were fascinated by chemistry, particularly with explosives. Anthony Randall joined Wargrave for the spring term; he was promptly nicknamed Harvey because one of my room-mates saw in him a likeness to Harvey the Invisible Hare, then appearing on the London stage. "Harvey" had a miniature cannon, for which he had been experimenting with homemade black gunpowder. It guttered and popped feebly. So he added potassium permanganate as an oxidant - now that at least gave a purple flash. Better! I suggested that powdered aluminium had certainly improved my experiments with Nicholas at home. He added some and tried again: there was a shattering bang, and the room filled with thick white smoke! It was not the sort of thing that the house prefects could ignore - they were on the scene in seconds. Then they withdrew for a rapid consultation: as he left, J.B.Pattinson turned and said quietly "Hide it all, quickly". We knew what would follow for sure. In less than a minute nothing was left of several illegal catapults, a .22 pistol and some ammunition, small bottles of spirits, cigarettes, a well thumbed copy of The Eunoch of Stamboul, and a large stock of chemicals. Anything that would not fit into hollow dictionaries was hidden under a loose floorboard. This included a dismantled 20 bore shotgun that normally lived in another boy's golfbag, used for illicit shooting on the Pevensey Marshes. (Their tame ferret remained undiscovered in the boiler room.) All through the house, the same desperate scramble was happening. When the Great

Arms Search followed, nothing was found but the cannon: the explosion was passed off as a trial with two starting pistol caps. It was not believed, but no other evidence was found.

Halfway through the Spring term, or Lent term as it was known, a major event happened. Everyone knew that our King, George the Sixth, was seriously ill. In fact he had most of one lung removed the previous year because of cancer, although I don't remember if the word was used. He was not a particularly impressive man, being a chain smoker with a severe stutter; but he was well respected, as he stepped up to the job when his playboy brother Edward insisted on marrying his divorced American mistress. That was not acceptable to the Church of England, of which he would have been the constitutional head. Britain generally felt that Edward had pushed philandering too far, and let the country down. (The schoolkids song of 1937 had been "Hark the herald angels sing - Mrs Simpson's pinched our King!") His circle, at least, had several prominent admirers of Hitler, and for this reason Edward was diplomatically sequestered in the Bahamas for the duration of the war. It is fair to say that King George was loved by the public for two things. One was for staying put in Buckingham Palace, a huge and obvious target, during the whole war. And the other was his practise of broadcasts to the nation, and indeed to the whole Empire as it was then, on Christmas Day. At that special time, he managed with a great effort to overcome his stutter, and in the darkest days of the war he managed to broadcast words of comfort to the split and bereaved families throughout the English speaking world. Now our reluctant King was dying. We got the news of his death in morning break. His young daughter Elizabeth, in her early twenties and recently married to a dashing Naval Officer - Phillip Mountbatten - returned rapidly to London from a holiday in Kenya. All the flags throughout Britain flew at half-mast for a week after the funeral. Phillip had been the popular commander of the Frigate HMS. Kelly, which was sunk under him during the siege of Malta. So with him and Princess Elizabeth the country suddenly had a generation change, from a succession of middle aged and elderly monarchs, going back to Queen Victoria, to a glamorous young couple. Everyone wished them well. The papers babbled about 'the New Elizabethan Age'. While it was hyperbole, the new feeling helped to shake off the aftermath of the war, and the grey days of nationalisation and rationing.

Easter

Something was missing: Dad's shotgun had always lived on the cupboards in the Big Room corridor. I asked Mother where it was. She said "You remember Mr Duprey, over on Pages Hill? Well, back in the winter things got too much for him.

His birds got the same disease that ours had last autumn. Like ours, they nearly all died. Their farm is smaller than ours, and they had smaller margins. He shot himself. Dad was terribly upset, as they were good friends. I thought it was safer to get rid of the gun." I thought of Mrs Duprey, and the five daughters. Lucy, the oldest, was a few months older than me. Pauline was the same age as Nonie. I was too shocked to speak.

Summer Term

A southern coastal town is a good place to be in summer. The weather is mostly warm, the trees are in full leaf, and the Downs looming above offer escape and freedom at times. The schedule of morning chapel and classes remained the same, but in the afternoons the classes followed lunch for three afternoons a week, then from four o'clock until prep we had cricket - or other games. And two days a week classes stopped at lunchtime. So the whole afternoon was given to sports, or sometimes to rambles in the countryside. I was even less use at cricket than at rugger. I could field, provided I was not too close-in; but I was little use as a batsman, as I could not face a rising ball. Afternoon sport became boring, then a waste of time.

We had a strange item of uniform for the summer term - a straw hat, which used to be called a boater - left-over items from Edwardian days. We called them 'bashers'. These were compulsory wear in town at all times. For the first few weeks we juniors felt horribly conspicuous in them, and crept around hoping nobody would notice them. Nobody did even appear to notice them, for the good reason that the whole town were much more used to seeing them than we were to wearing them! After a while we got used to them ourselves, and became even quite proud of them.

Beachy Head lighthouse from the Cliffs

On Sundays we would go up on the Downs to Beachy Head, and walk along the cliff tops to the point where you can look down on the famous light-house. The grass on the turf has got so used to being cropped by sheep that it never grows long. In summer it is full of thyme, and delicate blue flowers called harebells, whose stems are barely thicker than a hair. We would lie sheltered from the wind in the lee of the occasional thorn thickets, and read our books while idly watching the wind ruffling dark patches across the corn in the valleys. Over the sea the shadows of the little clouds seemed to chase each other across the waves, playing tag on their way to France over the horizon. When the south-west wind was blowing against the cliffs it caused an updraft so strong that the birds had great difficulty getting down to their nests. They would approach flying low over the grass: when they got to the cliff edge, they would suddenly tip beak-downwards, fold their wings, and slowly fall down against the wind. We used to try throwing stones over the cliff: they would get carried up by the wind, and fall far behind us. Trying to throw your basher away like that would sometimes result in it landing hundreds of yards inland.

Belle Toute Lighthouse from Beachy Head

The Corps

In the first year in the College, everyone was in the Army cadets. For one afternoon a week we began by learning drill; simply marching in step at first, then halting, marching off, then turns on the march, forming columns, and so on. Then we started rifle drill with .303 Lee Enfield rifles, which had been the infantryman's basic weapon in two World Wars. When we could march with rifles, we had to learn to strip and clean them, and learn how to do the same with a Bren gun, which is a fairly heavy but still portable field machine gun. We learned the basic organisation of the army, beginning with ordinary soldiers, (us), in Sections of about ten under a Lance Corporal. One Section of the three in a Platoon is led by a Corporal. The senior ranker in the Platoon is a Sergeant. Two or three platoons form a Company. As in the real army, in the cadets the senior ranks taught and drilled the newcomers. We also practiced 'Power of Command'. About eight cadets lined up along each side of the College field. Each boy, at the top of his voice, had to drill his opposite number fifty yards away above all the other commands and the noise of the traffic on the road. "We are training you to be leaders, not sheep. There are plenty of sheep. Your country needs officers, able to command, and to serve Britain and the Empire". The College was quite emphatic that it was not a military school. But a higher proportion of the boys joined the armed services than from some avowed military schools like Wellington. That was alright with me; I was going to be a naval officer.

By the end of the Summer term our little army was sent up to the Downs, where the Red Platoon attacked and the Blue Platoon defended a coppice of thorn bushes at the top of Paradise Wood. We painted our faces with khaki blanco, normally used for cleaning our webbing belts and gaiters, and stalked each other through the undergrowth firing blank ammunition. It was all good fun. My housemaster Major Tommy Rodd, who was in charge of the exercise, addressed us during our stale-bread and salami picnic. "Twelve years ago last month, when the Army was trying desperately to evacuate from the beaches at Dunkirk, and the Germans were already at the Channel coast, the sound of the guns could be heard from here. And the only soldiers here to defend Eastbourne were the College Cadet Force and a few members of the Home Guard. Some of them may have been your brothers or cousins. The rifles they held were the ones you are holding now. The difference, then, was that the bullets in the magazines were real ones. This may seem like fun, but we are teaching you in deadly earnest. We will change the roles of attackers and defenders. And remember, the time may come in only a few years when the boy who shows too much of himself may never hear the bullet that kills him - because it won't be a blank. This is for real. Now do it again. And I will be very severe with anyone who I can see out of cover." A much soberer army of fourteen year olds attacked and defended the redoubt of thorn bushes that afternoon.

Harebell

The First Year's End

At the end of the summer term the College put on an open day. I volunteered to operate a chemistry display: this was done by passing carbon dioxide gas over a lump of pure phosphorus under oil. When the gas came out into the air, it appeared to burn with a greeny-yellow flame. But the flame was cold to the

The Memorial Arch and tower

touch. I was proud of this, and thought it was fascinating. So apparently did the previous Wargrave housemaster's daughter Charmian. She was so interested that I showed her around all the other chemistry demonstrations too. My room-mate, Anthony Bavin (he of the shotgun and ferret), was less impressed. "Are you blind, you ass? It was you she found interesting - not the chemistry!" I hadn't noticed; and by then it was too late - she had gone.

The School Year ends in Speech Day. Our Sunday blue suits were worn to the Final Service, which unusually took place in All Saints Church, in order to accommodate all the pupils and most of their parents too. On our lapels we each wore a beautiful blue cornflower, which could well serve for the Sussex county flower at that time of year. Then everyone packed into Big School, the main assembly hall, for the Headmaster's Speech, and the award of the annual prizes for various academic or other distinctions, such as music or drama. The parents and masters then left, and the boys alone remained to watch the swearing-in of the first team colours for sports which had been awarded through the year. "I drink destruction to my enemies, and to myself also, if I do not fight on the field to the last drop of my strength. So help me." And a ritual quaff of Harvey's Ale followed. Stirring stuff. Since Victorian times the oath had been in Latin, but the rugger jocks so regularly got it wrong that recently a translation had been supplied in English. At least all concerned understood it, and were duly impressed. Then we sang the School Song, composed in Latin by an enthusiastic pseudo-traditionalist: Exultemus, O Sodales….. , or Rejoice, ye Sod-alls… as we preferred it! The classicists winced, but the days of their stranglehold over education were waning.

Woodbine and Galingale.

When I had cleared out the farm in the previous autumn (1951), Mr McCreadie at Galingale farm had offered to buy the chickens in the folds on the field I rented from him. He was aware that they had been sick. He employed a worker part time, who also worked at the much bigger Woodbine farm belonging to Mr Sam Cole. This worker also asked for permission to keep a small flock of his own at Galingale, and they were put in runs beside my ex flock. The worker was in daily contact with them and Woodbine Farm. In about June 1952 fowl pest was diagnosed at Woodbine, which actually borders on Galingale. Whether disease was transmitted by the worker or by proximity is unknown. But once again, the flock at Galingale, and the workers flock, were not apparently inspected, and were certainly not killed out. I was disgusted, and got the matter raised through the National Farmers Union, who were assured there would be an enquiry. As I pointed out, if these birds in direct contact were not removed, there would certainly be more trouble at Woodbine. Later Vet Hunter casually inspected my farm, without saying why. I do not know if he inspected Galingale; but the contact flock was certainly not killed out. Although Hunter had said there had never been a recurrence of fowl pest at a farm cleared up by the Ministry, in the next two years there were four more outbreaks at Woodbine.

Periwinkles

Waldron

Although so much in my life had changed, summer holidays still had that timeless quality. I helped on the farm, and things seemed to be going pretty well. My father was worried though, as there was an official outbreak of fowl pest at Woodbine

Farm, on Back Lane about half a mile away. But he said very little about it. I tried to corner the tractor driving jobs, and I had a schedule of paid jobs too, for pocket money. I had to work for my term-time spending money now.

My parents sometimes asked if I had any particular friends I wanted to invite home? Unlike my days at Tavistock, I found that the answer was no. I did not realise it until much later, but I think my reaction to the night and day pressure of boarding school, the compulsory sports, the sneering, and the hard work in class, was simply to keep civil with everyone if I could, but also to keep them all at arms length. I did not need allies, and I did not want friends in that atmosphere. I shared my interest in science and gadgetry, and I loved music, but I had nothing much to offer that the college boys valued. My parents said nothing.

Sailing With the Lord

A few boys at the College were members of a Christian youth group called the Crusaders. They used to have meetings on Sunday afternoons. I had better things to do with my Sundays, considering that there were already Matins in the morning and Choral Evensong in the early evening. That was my favourite service, as our main musical effort was devoted to anthems and Magnificats and vesper hymns for the Sunday evening. How Christian can you get? But the Crusaders organised a sailing camp on the Norfolk Broads, at Potter Heigham, during the summer holidays. And there for the first time we got out in sailing boats. I loved every minute of the sailing. The art of making a sailing boat do the apparently impossible, and use the wind to advance against the wind, was absolutely fascinating. Due to a misunderstanding between two tacking boats just below the infamous Potter Heigham Bridge, our first boat got stove-in and nearly sank! But that was the responsibility of the organisers, and nothing to do with me. We sailed all the way up the River Ant, tacking our Una-rig replacement boat for miles up the twisty river to Barton Broad. By the end of the week we had explored much of the Broads, and I had a new sporting hobby which was to become a lifelong passion.

But the Crusaders had another agenda. In the evenings they had religious meetings, with intense prayers for a few boys who were chronically sick, and for the salvation of everyone else. Either you were 'converted', and therefore 'saved'; or you were an outsider, an object of pity and slight misapprehension. After all, if Jesus loves you, and offers you eternal life in heaven singing simple little hymns with pleasant tunes, how can you refuse an offer like that? All you have to do is stand up and say "I am converted". So I did. Simple. But less simple than it appeared. Then of course you have to go and convert other people; and to do that you have to study the Bible intently, to be able to quote the relevant bits, so the word of God can win all your arguments for you. I wondered aloud why all this was necessary in addition to going to church? Then I found out there are many sorts of Christians, but the Evangelicals disapproved of all the others as only nominal believers, who respected the forms of religion without deeply doing enough about it. In a week I was pretty well brainwashed. Back at home I set about at least getting my parents to go to church more often. Maybe I could convert them? At least I ought to try, as I didn't want them to go to hell for ever. They sighed: then my mother said "We believe that God made the world. And farmers, more than most people, are very close to the way the world works. We feed our flocks, and what we produce feeds you and many more people besides. And if on Sunday we are tired and we work a little less hard, God said we should do so. So we think he understands, and will not send us to hell for not going to church too often. Because he looks at what we do, as much as what other self-righteous people may say." It may have been the longest speech I ever heard her make. I rather lost my evangelical zeal after that, and went back to my wicked ways of only going to chapel eight times a week during the autumn term.

Michaelmas

A new term: and only a twelve-month after starting in the dungeons of the first year I was already in the third year. Because I found sciences easy and enjoyable, I had now been promoted to the A sets. Our cohort had moved out of the Prep Room to more salubrious quarters, where we each had a small curtained cubicle for undisturbed work. Out of necessity we were being forced out of childhood's happy-go-lucky ways into doing an extra two hours study each day, with exercises to be delivered on time for marking by the masters. As the year went on, the pressure to be ready for O-Level went up notch by notch. Eastbourne was certainly teaching me how to work. Maybe if I had worked like this for the entrance scholarship exams, it would have made a big difference. And maybe I was a weed at sports, but my room-mates were sometimes turning to me for help with physics or chemistry 'prep'.

Already from my first term I had been studying the clarinet. Granny Brown wanted to pay for me to have music lessons. My initial trouble was not so much with getting notes out of the instrument - although it could produce alarming squeaks if not treated correctly. My real problem was in reading the music. I found if I could hear a piece played correctly, even if only once, I could commit it to memory and then play by ear. This modus operandi became a bad habit which is with me still: my sight reading is mediocre at best, but I have an excellent memory for music that I like.

Granny Brown made an event of my birthday in October every year. She was a very talented pastry cook, and loved to have an excuse to practice her arts. Dad and the whole family collected me from Eastbourne, and we drove up to Hailsham for a birthday tea that went on all afternoon. The table was covered in childrens delights: there were mince pies hot from the oven, there were fruit tarts, trifles, jellies, custard pies, cup cakes, ginger bread, and always a lovely layered birthday cake.

After the birthday tea Granny played her huge Bechstein grand piano for us - it took up half of her front room. She had studied music at the Royal Academy in London. She and her sister Patty used to sing duets and accompany other singers at concert parties as young women in Croydon. But she married my grandfather reluctantly, in order to reduce the burden on her own father, who had fallen into financial difficulties. And Grandpa Brown forbade her to play outside the house - he was a very strict Victorian, and found public performances unseemly and immoral. Even at home he had not liked her playing, so she had only played when he was out. We gave her an audience, and she played her heart out for us. There was the Warsaw Concerto, and Night on the Bare Mountain, Beethoven's Sonatas, and most amazing of all there was Chopin's Study on the Black Notes. We were all breathless at the end: she from exhaustion, being a frail little old lady; and us from holding our breath from the tension of it all! I returned to the college with as much of the feast as I could carry. And, while it lasted, I achieved a novel popularity in Wargrave.

I was by now fifteen, and my voice had broken. But because I was singing regularly, it didn't go wobbly or out of control. What happened was simply that I gradually gained additional notes in my lower register; the top notes of a boy treble were still there, but became harder to produce. As a result, I shifted from the trebles to the altos, which seemed a reasonable compromise. In fact, altos were in very short supply: there were only three of us in the choir, or even in the school Choral Society, which was practising for Handel's Messiah. This was so popular that half the College joined. We few altos had to sing the lead-in to the whole performance.

The autumn leaves turned gold, then brown, and had mostly fallen before the end of October. The weather became rainy and cold, and compulsory rugger became a dirty and increasingly miserable business; it was redeemed only by the steaming hot showers when we came back to the house. We rinsed off our filthy games kit, and tried to dry it before the next time we went out in the rain. The masters made light of it all. "Come on, this is only play. You'll all face worse than

this in the army! We are going to make men of you, somehow. So just shape up."
Eventually the Christmas holidays came. It was wonderful to get home to a warm
farmhouse. We had a white Christmas.

Cornflowers

Neighbours!

Our neighbour at Highlands Farm on the uphill side was now Major Julian Green,
an Irishman with red hair and a flaming short temper. He had taken over the
farm from the Durrants, and was raising pigs in the fields. Nonie told me of a
strange incident while I was away at school. "One day Julian's pigs broke through
the fence into A field, and started running wild. Dad, and Dave Fenner, tried to
drive them back. Of course Sherry and Simon joined in too. They had managed
to get the pigs back to the top of the field when Julian arrived, and a furious row
broke out. Ignoring the fact it was his pigs that had done the damage, he shouted
'You Sir, your dogs and your servants, are not without your nuisance value!'" But
the pigs had broken the wire netting of the poultry runs, and the breeding hens
escaped. Before order was restored the hens had got into some unused henhouses
that had not been cleaned up since the last outbreak.

Before long the old symptoms appeared around the farm again.

I do not know whether the infection came from the old hen houses or the surviving flock at Galingale 150 yards away. But 'colds' broke out among the birds in this field, the egg production dropped suddenly, and some birds died with marked darkening of the head. Similar problems very soon occurred in the brooder house. Desperately worried, because of my previous experience, I again notified the MoA in Lewes. Vetinary Officer MacDonald came, who had never before been to the farm. He made a thorough investigation. I made no mention of the previous history, wishing this to be judged on its merits. He placed a standstill order on the farm. He did a PM on a bird, and found a haemorrhage in the lining of the gizzard, and seemed to think it was serious. He seemed very helpful and pleasant, saying he understood that I had reported trouble before, and that there had been trouble in East Sussex ever since. When I then told him of my previous loss of 5000 birds he was appalled, and said "Of course the Ministry will help you - that's what we are here for".

Vet Hunter - who had failed last summer to carry out the investigation requested through the NFU - 'just happened to be passing by', and asked if it was my intention once again to kill out the stock at my own expense? It was patently obvious that someone at the Ministry was hoping for just this. I was furious. I said it was ridiculous to suggest that a breeder should do this if the farm hadn't got pest; and if it had, then the Ministry should do it, and accept their responsibilities. Later Hunter came back, and said he was taking over the case, as MacDonald was called away. He said that the current fowl pest symptoms were largely nervous, with twitching necks and partial paralysis. I did not know this, but I had seen some cases. When I found one and showed it to him, he said nothing at all. In an obvious attempt to impress me, he took a lot of blood samples. It would be interesting to know what really happened to these samples taken from my farm.

The Regional Veterinary Supervisor, a Mr Black, tried to allay my (non-existent) suspicion that someone at the Testing Lab had interfered with the samples, as they were sent under coded identification. I suppose it would be much easier to do any interference at Lewes, though the thought did not occur to me until Black raised it!

The Great Freeze

January came and went, with little outdoor sport possible, as the pitches were mostly covered with snow. I used to play squash at the club on the other side of College Road. At least it was properly heated. Then in February the weather took a sharp turn for the worse. After a heavy snowfall, the wind turned to the east. People said it came straight from Russia; and for once what people said was literally correct. There was a blocking anticyclone over the Ural mountains; and the wind blew unhindered from the Steppes of Siberia, across the Baltic and North Seas, to us.

Nowadays, when many children start skiing before their sixth birthday, it seems surprising that I was fifteen before I even saw anyone skiing. Someone holding two sticks was moving extraordinarily fast just above the golf links at the far end of Paradise Drive - skiing on the South Downs at sea level in Sussex! Two of the girls from the Chelsea College of Physical Education had obviously enjoyed a wider education than ours. The whole country was snowbound. I phoned my father, and he sent our heavy farm sledge down by train on 'The Cuckoo Line', which ran from Eridge, via Heathfield, down to Polegate and so to Eastbourne Station. I dragged the sledge on the ice back up South Street. Sledging the Downs became an acceptable substitute for compulsory rugby, as the playing fields were harder than rock. My sledge was popular, as it cut through the snow and was quite rapid. But you had to turn it and stop before the last bank above the Links. One of my house mates (it may have been John Chitty) had a frighteningly fast machine - a little luge made from a frame over the tips of two broken skis. You could say it was a runaway success, until it went so fast it flew right over the bank out into about twenty feet of empty air, and was crushed below him on landing. The same afternoon I lent my sledge to a study-mate who was rather prone to day-dreaming. In spite of careful instructions, he appeared entranced with the sheer downhill thrill, didn't even try to turn, and landed on the Links underneath the sledge. He went to hospital with concussion, and was gone for the rest of the term. Although I wasn't blamed, sledging stopped that evening.

But the freeze got steadily colder every day; and even worse, every night. The Wargrave Upper Cubes dormitory had three and a half uninsulated outside walls, not to mention the roof, and the two radiators were unequal to the task. The water pipes froze indoors. We first wore two pairs of pyjamas, then two pairs of socks in bed (unheard-of behaviour), then we put our fire-drill rugs on the beds, followed by our dressing gowns, followed by a pile of all our clothes. We ended up by wearing our games kit under our pyjamas. No-one actually got frostbite. But the night I borrowed the Physics lab's maximum/minimum thermometer it registered seventeen degrees Fahrenheit indoors the next morning. For Alaskan fur trappers, sleeping in the snow, that would have been what they call 'a three dog night.' It really was phenomenally cold for England - particularly for Sussex.

After three numbingly cold weeks the wind pattern finally changed. The weather warmed, and torrents of rain began melting the snow. With the rivers already in flood, the highest tide of the year coincided with an onshore gale both in East Anglia and Holland. The rivers flowing to the sea were blocked, and the dykes gave way: both the rivers and the sea itself overwhelmed the coastal defences, and thousands were drowned on both sides of the North Sea. Our complaints about the weather began to seem very petty. England was stunned.

Following Vet Hunter's visit, a number of chick carcasses were sent to the Ministry Weybridge Laboratory for PM tests., which found sinusitis and thickening of the air sacks, and stating "Certain other post mortem findings indicated a possible infection with Newcastle Disease (fowl pest) virus." Arrangements were made for further blood tests. The farm was under a standstill order, and I was unable to take in fresh stock or to sell birds which were ready for the market. After waiting for several days I phoned the Ministry at Lewes to ask if they had the blood test results. Mr Burns replied that they were all clear; and I asked if that meant that I could move stock? He asked what I wanted to do? "I want to get on with my business and sell stock". "How do you propose to sell them?" "Any way I want, alive or dead. I know what this means, and I intend to clear out my birds as quickly as I can." He became annoyed. "What about anyone else buying them?" "If there is nothing wrong on my farm, it cannot be passed to anyone else". "In that case we shall keep you closed down for as long as we can". The standstill order was kept on for a month, and the five week loss of the chicks intake caused serious losses to my production. After the withdrawal of Vet MacDonald, the Lewes vets showed a complete disinterest in actively helping the farm, being concerned only to shutdown operations here.

Geography

During my college days J.P Underhill, nicknamed 'Pot', was the housemaster of Blackwater; he was also Senior Geography Teacher, and a legend in his own time.

I was fiddling under the desk in the evening geography class with some newly acquired gadget, when there was a shattering crash: an iron tipped arrow was quivering in the desk less than a foot in front of me. "What was the last thing I said?" I closed my eyes briefly to try to remember. Something started whistling rhythmically above me. I raised my eyes to see that he was swishing a nine foot long pole, used as a blackboard or map pointer; the upswing stopped just below the ceiling, and the downswing ended about halfway down my nose. Pot, like many teachers, hated inattention!

One day it was my turn to read the morning lesson from chapel. I stood up, and started reading. "Brown! You are mumbling, boy. Hold your head up. More!" I tried, and continued reading. Pot left his podium, and went wandering around the classroom, as he frequently did. There was a little noise behind me, and something pressed upwards gently, then firmly, under my chin. Pot was standing behind me: I swivelled only my eyes downwards to see that he was holding in both hands - an Indian war tomahawk! "Now, go on with the lesson" Pot's collection of artefacts and weapons was not only impressive - he could use them too, on occasions.

English

The College as a whole had a collective obsession with pronunciation. The greatest abhorrence was felt for the thin and nasal Kent and Sussex pronunciation of 'ow'. Nice raound 'aows' were required: any hint of 'eeow' was anathema. As a country boy, I was called Breeaown for two years to underscore the point. The correction campaign was led by 'Pimp' Halliday, a modern languages master. Offenders were sent to recite an odd number - typically seventeen -'brown cows' to a trusted member of the languages sixth form: "There are thousands and thousands of brown cows, prowling round about the grounds." Another abomination was the elision of words, particularly those ending in the letter 'r'. Offenders had to recite 'raw eggs': "I saw a raw egg in the drawing room obeying the law of gravity". Any suggestion of rawr-eggs or drawring or lawr-of was scathingly put down.

A newer member of staff, Mr 'Bouncy' Barrett was the second music teacher, a genial soul, with however two notable characteristics. One was his long high-springing stride: he bounced down the Cloisters in a way that only Tibetan monks do when covering long distances in a hurry. The other was a thin nasal

Sussex "Bee-eounce" to his proneeounciayetion! The masters took turns to read the chapel lessons in Sunday Evensong - the main ecclesiastical event of the week. So, when his turn came around it was rumoured to be an interesting subject. I think we all looked up the text. O Glory! "And the peeower of the Lord shone reeound abeeout him". Four hundred and six smirking faces ducked behind their respective pews in unison, while the masters struggled to keep straight faces. Poor man.

The School Train

For some reason Dad could not collect me in the Ute at the end of term. I think he was laid up again with an inflamed throat. So I came home instead on the School Train. This is a venerable institution at boarding schools. A Special train ran through central Sussex up the Cuckoo Line, stopping at nearly all stations to Eridge, then on to Croydon and Victoria in London. The Southern Railway usually laid on a smart Schools class 4-4-0 steam locomotive to haul us. The boys were out of school uniform, and many of them smoking like chimneys. It was a fairly rowdy gang on the train, as schoolboy horseplay had a short fling, singing loudly the few rude songs we knew. With whistle blowing, the Special turned away from the main line at Polegate, and we steamed on our toilet-roll-unfurling way with bugles blowing Reveille through Hailsham, Horam-for-Waldron, Hellingly Halt, and on to Heathfield. And - for me - back to the land.

Easter

At home for the holidays, Penny said there had been more trouble with our neighbour Julian. He had a dog, an old fashioned English Bull Terrier, white with a piratical black patch over one mad pink eye; a nasty bit of work. Penny said it waited for her and Nonie coming home from school, and growled and sometimes chased them. One day it came right into our house, and threatened Mother in the hall. My father phoned Julian to take his dog home, and Penny said "I never heard such a row, or heard Dad so furious. Julian raged about 'people who didn't understand dogs'. Dad said that if he could not control a dangerous animal, and let it threaten neighbours in their own homes, he deserved to be prosecuted."

I gathered also that Patrick, my innocent looking young brother, was turning out less innocent than he looked. Even when he was three or four, he maintained that he had a secret friend - his cousin Owzie who lived in Norwork - and would sometimes quote Owzie on various subjects. We tried to jolly him out of this. I suppose a more psychological family nowadays would have understood that it was a way of saving some pride from a family in which he was always the youngest and the least informed. Now he had made friends with Crispin McCredie, a neighbours son, and they had been found smoking a carefully collected selection of dog-ends in a clay pipe!

Mother told me, with a half smile, "Oh, and Bumper Humphries died last month. Dad was going to send a wreath of chicken feathers! I had to stop him."

The Seven Sisters from Cuckmere Haven

Summer Days

The early summer term celebrated two religious holidays. We had a half day for Ascension Day, and a full holiday for Whitsun. We took a picnic, and went off into the countryside for a peaceful time, alone or with friends. I took a good book, and went up as far away as I could, on the Downs towards Belle Tout lighthouse, now disused and replaced by the Beachy Head lighthouse at the foot of the cliffs.

The best day out was undoubtedly Regatta Day. The College Rowing Club was a favoured alternative to cricket in the summer term. They kept their boats at Cuckmere Haven, and rowed on the twisty waters of the old course of the Cuckmere, the little Sussex river that is a perfect geography lesson in wandering rivers and Oxbow Lakes.

The river is so narrow that the skiffs cannot possibly race side by side, so the pairs and fours raced in tandem, each with its own start and finishing posts. Despite this problem, the College usually did pretty well at the annual Marlow Regatta. Our own Regatta was mostly races between House Teams. But we all went over to the Cuckmere for the day with our packs of sandwiches and bottles of ginger beer. It was haymaking time. On the other side of the river an old Fordson was mowing. The air was redolent of cowpats, tall grass, new-mown hay, and the distant aromatic odour of tractor kerosene. High overhead a couple of kestrels soared and hovered, looking for field mice or rabbits, turned out of their nests by the mower. One College boy had a specially adapted basher for Regatta Day. The crown was cut around almost to the back, and a fine string was led up the back and over the top of the crown to the front. Instead of raising it to people he met, at a pull on the string the crown raised itself like the lid of a bean can, and underneath a large text said 'A very good day to you'. It was too.

Vincent "Vim" Allom

Decades later, I am still wondering how Vim taught so much while not appearing to teach at all. Traditionally for schoolboys, we sat at the back of the class. So he perched on a desk somewhere in front of us, and simply engaged us in intelligent conversation. He was always interested in rather marginal topics; we learned that the masters were fascinated by the boys nicknames for them. He also sounded out our opinions on many things; sports results and prospects for the rest of the season; politics and what was happening to the country, parallels with history, the College during the war, and so on. I realise now that, by discussing things we knew about or which interested us, he was leading us on to speak coherently in public. We simply thought we were having a good time. Just occasionally he would sound us out about literature, or even better - he would read to us. No-one in his class ever failed English language or literature exams; we simply absorbed the subject by example. His statement once on religions in general raised eyebrows. "I suppose, if I were to take religion seriously, I would have been a Buddhist." It had never occurred to any of us at the time that you had any choice in such matters! He was not a snuff addict, rather I think it was a quirk - a social affectation nearly two centuries after its time. He kept a little silver snuffbox in his trouser pocket; during a lapse in the flow of events, or more notoriously during a Sunday sermon of which he chose to disapprove, he would produce the box and tap it gently. Then he would sprinkle a pinch of snuff onto the back of his hand, raise it to each nostril in turn, and sniff powerfully. Once, to entertain us, he rolled up his sleeve and sprinkled snuff from elbow to finger tip, before inhaling the lot in one sweeping movement. At least he did not do that in his choirstall!

Exams

Half of the school was working for exams. My year were studying as never before for GCE O-Levels. In order to keep people to a reasonable number of subjects, the edict was that you could only sit for eight. Reluctantly, I dropped French. Failing to see my name on the lists, my French master put it back. The seniors were sitting their A-Levels, and the school seemed unusually hushed and serious. I was very impressed when our own turn came. We were ushered into Big School, the formal heart of the College, to sit at well separated rows of desks. Masters and others sat on the stage, keeping a beady eye on proceedings. The exam papers were laid face down on our desks. Then "This is the O-Level Additional Mathematics 1 exam. You have two hours. Answer question 1, and any five others. Turn your papers over now." The oak panelled walls, each panel with an individually painted heraldic shield, stared unsympathetically back if I ever looked up. It was amazing how the time flew. Outside, the occasional thunk of willow on leather spoke of cricket practice in the nets. Mostly the questions had been forseen, and well enough covered in class. Tom Rodd, my housemaster, was a brilliant predictor of questions. "Gentlemen, there is no substitute for knowing the whole syllabus. Assuming that you already know that, then any additional revision of the following topics would probably be found worthwhile." His predictions, revised between the first and second Chemistry exams, were generally about eighty percent accurate. I felt quietly confident about my prospects. Generally the rule was that all the A set and most of the B set passed any subject; C sets still had a fighting chance, while D sets would be surprised to see a pass. When the results arrived later, I had got seven subjects, failing Latin. In that I was in good company, as half the A set failed, along with all the other candidates. The Latin exam was an aberration. Oxford and Cambridge still required O-Level Latin with your A-Levels. The fact that the other seventeen Universities in Britain had no such rule went un-noticed in academe and career planning. The November Latin 'retake' was a giveaway in compensation. But I didn't sit for it. I was going to take the Dartmouth Royal Navy exam in the autumn. As far as the College was concerned, failing Latin meant that I could not go to University. I didn't care; I was going to join the Navy.

During the spring and early summer I managed to keep the farm going. Growth rates were disappointing, but mortality seemed within acceptable bounds. I hoped that the stock would build a natural resistance to this disease, whatever it was. I got a prescription from a private vet for the use of penicillin antibiotic. However the growth rate dropped steadily and the mortality rose. I realised it would soon be impossible to continue; and not wishing to experience the same victimisation from Lewes again, I contacted a newly formed independent body, The Animal Health Trust. I sent specimens and a description of the symptoms. They replied saying that they suspected fowl pest, and had contacted the MoA in Lewes. The farm was again placed under a standstill order. A Ministry vet arrived from Lewes, and after inspecting the birds remarked "Well, I suppose that we shall have to go through the whole rigmarole again." Blood samples were taken. I suppose they were 'alright', because the standstill order was promptly lifted. Having no confidence at all in this, I took further samples myself, and sent them to the AHT laboratory. They said that only the Ministry could do the blood test. So I sent further samples myself to the Ministry lab in Weybridge.

A few days later Vet Hunter came from Lewes in a great rage. He stormed and raved that I had no right to send in blood tests myself. This infuriated me. "I have made my living here for twenty years, before your people left this foul infection on my doorstep." I then asked "Are the blood samples alright?" First of all he hedged. I bluntly repeated, "I asked - are they alright?" Very uncomfortably, he said "Yes, they were. What are you making such a fuss about?" I stated that it was ruinous to go on like this. The respiratory infections (confirmed by PMs) had never been recognised by the MoA vets, and the trouble was steadily getting worse. I considered that I had every right to have the tests made, and if they were indeed satisfactory, I intended to have a sale and clear out all of the birds. I had no intention of losing 5000 head of stock like the last time. He then became calmer, inspected the farm, and agreed that the older birds indeed looked seriously sick. But nothing was done.

By now I did not believe a word I was told by the Lewes vets. Of course, they were putting on a bold front. But while I felt that this was so, I could not be sure. All the time I kept asking myself why, why, why? Although I knew they were treating my case differently from others, I could not think of any possible motive. Mr Cole, not half a mile away, had been cleaned up and compensated, so why not me? I reasoned that if my trouble really was fowl pest, the Lewes vets would not dare to let me have a sale. Even up to the morning of the sale, I expected it to be stopped. A local girl who worked in the Ministry office in Lewes, remarked to someone that there was trouble at our place, and the sale ought not to go on. I was told long afterwards that nearly every buyer complained bitterly to the Auctioneers, and some threatened to take action. Poor Mr Cole had been told by phone that he would be free from restrictions from his last outbreak on that day. He bought birds at my sale, and as he was unloading them he was met by the vet bringing the lifting order. When the vet heard where he had bought them, he was prosecuted for breaking the terms of his standstill order! Naturally, his farm went down for its fourth outbreak a few weeks later. Three other buyers of our stock gave up poultry in disgust, and concentrated on dairy or arable farming.

A Naval Summer

The Coronation happened during the summer term. The whole country had a special holiday, and I went home for a long weekend. London was filled with pageantry, which we watched on television somewhere. And Waldron village organised a sports day on the cricket pitch, followed by a meal for everyone in the village hall.

This was followed shortly afterwards by a ceremonial Fleet Review of the Royal Navy. We still had a large Navy; and about a hundred ships, from battleships down to submarines, were drawn up and anchored in a huge array in the Spithead Channel off Portsmouth. In a pale blue dress, our young Queen stood alone on the bridge of a Frigate that solemnly sailed past every ship of the Fleet, taking the salutes as it went. By this time I had moved from the Army recruits to the Naval Section of the Corps. We put on our uniforms for the occasion, and went by coach down to Portsmouth, where we could see the distant anchored ships, and watch a close-up on the TV.

At the beginning of the summer holidays the Corps went to their annual camp. This meant a week in tents for the Army. For us in the Naval Section, we went that year for a week in HMS Vanguard, Britain's last remaining battleship. Although these ships are huge and heavily armed, modern warfare had already made them more of a liability than an asset, as they were too easy to attack and destroy from the air. But Vanguard was an impressive beast. Hugely long and surprisingly lean, armed fore and aft with enormous sixteen inch guns capable of firing the width of the English Channel, she even had an elegant sheer to the deckline resembling that of a yacht. She was still in commission - just - although no-one really supposed she would ever be used again. We twenty cadets were housed in one of the boy-seamen's messes somewhere below decks. The whole surroundings were steel, walls ceilings doors and floors, all painted cheerful light green or cream. Machinery hummed night and day. We slept in hammocks: that is to say we tried to sleep. A hammock is a very uncomfortable bed. Before six in the morning a bosun's pipe would shrill throughout the ship. Petty officers would appear in the doorway, shouting "show a leg - lash and stow!" By which they meant "roll-up your hammocks" and stow them in wire bins for the day, liberating the mess for dining tables and exercise space. Then we were sent above for scrubbing decks. One of my memories is holystoning the deck of HMS Vanguard as the sun rose over the docks, with the surprisingly warm seawater of Portsmouth Harbour gushing from the hose and pouring over my bare feet. Against expectations, I found it quite enjoyable!

Once again, I managed to put my foot in it - or rather on it. A Petty Officer (the naval equivalent of a Sergeant) was instructing us in 'swinging the lead', which is the way you drop a lead-line to take depth soundings from a moving ship. You have to throw the lead - a ten pound steel weight - well in front of the ship, so that it is on the sea-bottom when the ship passes over it. So you swing the lead backwards and forwards in ever bigger arcs until you can swing it around in a full circle. Then at eight o'clock on a forward rising arc you release the line, and the lead flies out well in front of the bows. Standing there on Vanguard's high bow, I got a big circle going, and released my hold just right. I felt a sudden jerk underfoot, the line snapped under the shock, the lead flew high into the air, and sank forever to the bottom of Portsmouth Harbour. My Petty Officer's language was quite educational!

Michaelmas Prospects

I was headed for the Navy Exams in November, which meant that my academic life was put on the back burner. I was moved into the Services Fifth, a special form which shared some classes with the Fourth Year, a category reserved for those who had failed O-Levels. Looking around, I noticed that my class-mates all conformed to a certain type. They were fit, good at sports such as rugger cricket and boxing, alert, obedient, and very unlikely to get into trouble - good prefect material in fact. And academically most of them would have found the B-sets pretty taxing. By the end of the first week I found I was bored, and rather disappointed too. I took the fifth form maths classes to keep my hand in, as the Navy had higher standards than the others. I put my efforts into music for that term. I moved from the Junior Orchestra to the main School Orchestra with my clarinet. And I joined the Corps of Drums, a bugle and drum band in the cadets. This was definitely an elite group within the Corps; and there was the usual sneering that they would take a weed. But the drums ran completely independently of the staff; the experienced drummers and buglers taught the newcomers, and it was a great feeling to lead the whole school on marches and parades.

The Navy exams happened in the middle of autumn. I went up to London to stay with 'Aunty' Sylvia Nairn, who had sold us Simon and Sherry. She had a small Mews flat somewhere in Kensington, and I had to master the Underground to go daily to an examination hall somewhere in the City. During the time I was there London had one of the infamous 'pea-souper' fogs. Most houses were heated with coal fires: the belching smoke from the chimneys was trapped by the stagnant air. It was a good thing that I had two clear days to learn the way home, because by the Friday you could barely see across the street. The air was choking with soot and sulphur: even indoors the air was so thick that there was a faint halo around every light bulb, sparkling dimly like a dirty rainbow. I returned gratefully to Sussex and clean air. When the body-counts were finally done some weeks later, they calculated that the 'Great Smog' had killed well over four thousand people that week. When the exam results arrived, one fifth of the candidates had passed: I was halfway down the pass list. I had been fairly confident so far; but everyone at home and on the staff were very pleased.

Next came the interviews, and these were to happen at the famous Britannia Royal Naval College at Dartmouth. We gathered first in London for a medical examination, including eyedrops which completely messed up my vision for hours. Then a party of ten candidates was sent down to Devon by train. We arrived at Kingswear station in the evening, and I was intrigued that we were taken to the College in an open motorboat across the River Dart. The College is a big imposing building in white stone and red brick, halfway up the hill opposite. Inside is even more striking: everywhere seemed to be golden wood panelling. The place was apparently run by Petty Officers, and everyone ran everywhere at the double. I don't think I saw anyone at all walking. Next morning we were briefly interviewed. Then we were taken to a big gymnasium for initiative tests. A variety of arrangements were made of ropes, beams, boxes, jumping horses, tyres and falling mats. One by one we each had to look at the equipment, and then command the remaining nine candidates in crossing an obstacle, such as a 'river' marked on the floor. We most of us succeeded after a fashion. At the end of the afternoon we were lined up, and the results were announced there and then. Two were sent 'to have their particulars took', and the rest of us were simply thanked for coming. And that was it. It took a couple of minutes to sink in: I had failed. I cannot remember that evening, or much about the journey home. I was simply blank, I couldn't feel anything; not even disappointment at first. I had no alternative plans as I had no other ambitions. Ever since I was a little boy I had been going to join the Navy: it had never occurred to me that they might not take me. Looking back, I think that the steady sneering had worn away my original self-confidence, so I did not project the necessary authority to be officer material.

Eastbourne took the news in a very matter-of-fact way. Tom Rodd said, "Well, there is another entrance exam at seventeen plus, before A-Levels. You had better go back to the A-Level classes, and catch up half a term's work again". Dad said very little; but Mother was bitterly disappointed. The fact was that, had the Navy taken me, they would also have taken over my running costs. And this mattered more than I realised.

1954

Winter

By now my farm had been completely cleared out three times; in the late summer of 1950 after severe losses, again in December 1951 after losing 5000 out of 6000 birds, and now in October 1953 after the sale of everything fit to move. The farm had only had less than a year of proper operations during this period. So we had all the economic costs, and very little proper returns. I was deeply in debt to the millers, and to a number of other suppliers. Jack Newnham the miller was one of my oldest friends, and he was very understanding. I had originally intended, when we re-started in February 1952, to get the farm running again and then sell it as a going concern. It had been valued as worth around £12,000 at that time. Then our plan was to take the family and emigrate to Victoria in Australia. Yet when the stock was healthy, the farm made money at an impressive rate. So we decided to carry on. My hope was that, even after this further set-back, with healthy stock the debts and overdrafts could be paid-off in a reasonable time. The farm was mortgaged to the bank, and some further operating capital was raised from my mother, and also from Alan (Tommy) Bonfield, my brother-in-law. The funds were administered by an accountant, who paid all the bills and received all the payments. I had a rather small 'wage' from the accountant for running the farm. It was inflexible and humiliating, but it was the only way to continue in business, and the only chance to win clear of my debts to the creditors and to my relations.

The poultry houses were steam cleaned and re-stocked in February 1954, and all seemed to be going well. The returns were indeed so impressive that the accountant proposed joining the business as a partner, and offered to put in considerable capital.

The Social Season

Our family were growing up. I was sixteen, Nonie was rising fourteen, and Mother wanted us to have the sort of social life and friends that had been the norm in the golden days - as it seemed - of their youth in the nineteen twenties. So we had a party in the Big Room. A nice crowd of about twenty young guests was invited, with friends for each of our ages. We had some very good party food, and some of the traditional party games too, like the version of hide-and-seek known as 'sardines', and blindfold games where when blindfolded you have to identify someone else by touch, and so on. Then we had some dancing, and at last we could make serious use of the skills learned years before in the Cross-in-Hand village hall. I remember clearly, while going to change the record for a 'Gentleman's Invitation' waltz, I said loudly "I bags Jane Smythe". Nonie was rightly scandalised. "Robin, you'll do no such thing! Jane may dance with you, but you must ask her nicely first - like a Gentleman". Ouch! But she was quite right. And indeed she did dance with me. It was sometime later, I was invited to her house for a polite tea; and we were playing records in the lounge afterwards. One of the songs was an unusual one of George Formby, playing a Spanish Guitar for the song of the Lancashire Toreador. It was a good song; but I just loved the sound of the guitar. My romance-to-be was not Jane, but the Spanish Guitar.

That same Christmas holiday I was invited to another much bigger dance for teenagers, given by four families somewhere over Hailsham way. They even had a small band playing for about sixty of us kids. And there I met a girl of about fourteen or fifteen called Jane Ross-Lowe. She had a royal blue dance dress, and jet black hair in a shoulder length bob. But the fascination was her smiling dark eyes, like deep forest pools, that locked mine so I could not look away. I had never had a girl friend: I had not even thought I wanted one - until that evening. But I did not know what to do about it. So the dance broke up, we were all collected and driven home - and I was left with something else to think about.

Pixie

Winter, or Lent, term was very different from last year's. The weather was mild, and Eastbourne introduced hockey for the first time. And here was a sport at last where size was not the winning formula. In fact being small was an advantage, as you could manoeuvre more quickly. Flexible wrists counted for more than brute strength, and I was sufficiently fast to do quite well. At last, I had found a field sport that I could actually enjoy.

But it was about this time that the College got savagely beaten by our traditional rivals Radley at rugger. There was a love-hate relationship with Radley College, as Eastbourne had been closed down and evacuated there for much of the war after Dunkirk. There had been two depleted schools operating in parallel in one set of buildings in Hertfordshire, which was not in the immediate path of the expected German invasion. So they were natural opponents in all the field sports, as much as they were allies in the classrooms. This lived on in a fierce rivalry a decade later. Our Headmaster took the defeat very personally, and decided to administer a shock to the whole of the College. "You are all half-asleep, in class and on the field" he told us. So the whole school had to be at work by seven a.m, for half an hour of extra prep. At the same time Captain Rogers of the Royal Marines reformed our genial morning PT. We had to go back to our houses for a very tough session of Marines exercises in games kit. It did more good in ten minutes than our trot-around had done in thirty. "Do these few exercises every day for the rest of your life" he told us, "and you will live ten years longer". By my late thirties, this looked like a bargain: I am still keeping my side of it!

We chatted for a few minutes after going to bed in our dormitory. Something another boy had said weeks before suddenly rang a bell in my memory. "Geof, does your sister still have the pony?" "Yes, and Dad is worried, because we will soon have no-one to look after her." "I think I may have a solution for you". Since she was six, Nonie had wished on every new moon and every falling star to have a pony of her own. Next day, I phoned home, and put the idea to my parents. "Pixie is nearly sixteen, and has only a few more years of riding left". "Never mind," said Dad, " We have plenty of grass and a stable, and I know someone who will be delighted".

The Scandal

It had happened shortly before my time, in about 1949 or 1950. But the topic haunted us for years. Girlfriends were always officially discouraged, though not quite forbidden outright to seniors. Forbidden fruit has a special attraction; in this case the girls of the Eastbourne Domestic Science College were enthusiastic collaborators. Five or six college seniors from School House used to take some of the 'Cookers' out to the cafes of Seaside late in the evenings. They got back into their residence by climbing a convenient drainpipe. Unfortunately for Cupid, the drainpipe had weak mountings: one night as the college boys climbed back down, the pipe and the boys fell with a crash into the road. Windows flew open, the police were called, one of the boys was injured and was taken to hospital. The press got hold of the story, and Eastbourne remained 'The Scandal School' for most of my time there.

In the Post

It was towards the end of the term. I was assembling my books for the morning classes when Anthony Bavin appeared at my side. "You have a letter from some woman". The morning post was laid out on the main hall table by the front door at 8.30 am, just before we had to leave for chapel. And there indeed was a blue Basildon Bond envelope addressed to me. I looked at it: the writing was the careful round hand of a well educated girl. Bavin must have had a very practised eye. He didn't say much, but he was acutely aware of the opposite sex. I put it in my pocket; to open later, away from the curious gaze of my room-mates. It was addressed from the Sanatorium of Moira House, the neighbouring girls school. And signed Jane.(Ross-Lowe). She was in the San with flu', out from under the eagle eyes of the mistresses, and feeling daring too. Well then, I didn't have to do anything: it was done for me! All I had to do was to write back.

Easter Holidays

Pixie was a resident at the farm before I even got home for Easter. She came free with her saddle and all her tack, against just the promise of a good home; and she changed my sisters' lives. She was a lively pony, belying her age; a dark bay with one white sock. And she had hidden talents. She had been a gymkhana pony all her life, and she knew the games and competitions of the ring better than her riders. She had a particular knack, in that she could turn towards the forefoot that she was putting down. Most horses find this impossible; and it made Pixie almost unbeatable in the 'bending' races. Nonie said "All you have to do is sit tight and hang on till she delivers you to the finishing line!" Before long Pixie was joined by Gunner, a lazy ex-army horse belonging to a friend of Nonie's.

Patrick had caused some concern last term when one of the Tavistock teachers had called in, wondering when he would be sufficiently well to return to school, as end of term exams were approaching. It seems that for nearly three weeks he had left every morning, bought a snack with his lunch money, and disappeared down into Tavistock woods for the whole day! I suppose it was private enterprise, in solving his problems by himself. But it was worrying that he hadn't felt able to tell anyone that he was unhappy.

The farm was now in full production again, and seemed to be flourishing. Most of the stock were being raised as table birds. The cleanliness and disinfection were fanatical. The old women who came to pluck the chickens remarked "Why, at Mr Armstrong Brown's farm, you could eat straight off the floor!"

Romance - of Sorts

I looked up the name in the East Sussex telephone book. There could be no doubt; Ross-Lowe, Coldharbour Farm, Hellingly. I spent several days in a sweat, nerving myself to make the phone call. Finally I called the operator, gave the number, and waited. A woman's voice replied. "Can I speak to Jane please?" "I think she's in; I'll call her", and further away "Pom - phone". Then silence. I waited two minutes, then three. Just when I was about to give up in disappointment, I thought I heard someone breathing. I said "Is someone there?" "Yes, it's me - Jane". "It's me - Robin". "I hoped you would call." "I got your letters, did you get mine?" So we arranged that I would cycle over that afternoon for a family tea. I cleaned myself up, to the accompaniment of some snickering from my sisters; then I set off for a several mile cycle ride to Hellingly, almost to Hailsham. Coldharbour was a serious looking tall house in a dark knoll of pine trees at a bend in the road. I went to the door, and was met by Jane's mother. "I remember you, you were at the party weren't you?" She was a tallish woman in her mid forties, well spoken , wearing rugged country clothes. If I was the object of any curiosity, it didn't show at all. Tea was in the large farmhouse kitchen. Jane came in, looked cautiously at me, and smiled a bit nervously. Her older sister came in, whose name I already knew. She had had a rather wild romance with one of the senior boys at the college, until an intercepted letter gave away much too much of the game and became a considerable scandal. She seemed normal and nice enough to me. After the meal Jane and I went off on our bikes, and walked awhile along the banks of a little river. Casually, as if it was the most natural thing, I took her hand and held it. Then we walked back again, cycled back to the house, and said goodbye. We stood there for a moment, just looking at each other. I ought to have kissed her. But I didn't know how to ask. So I did not get one.

But next term, the letters started again. We graded them carefully, keeping step. 'Dear,' My Dear', 'Dearest'; and 'Love', 'My Love': and in the well understood progression we had just got to 'My Dearest' and 'All my love' when we were betrayed. Tommy Rodd summoned me to his study. "I have received a letter from Miss Swan." There was no need to explain; she was the founder and legendary headmistress of Moira House. "It seems you have been corresponding with one of her pupils." "I did not know it was against the College Rules Sir". (I knew damn well it was not). He sighed. "It is inappropriate behaviour. It may not be explicitly against our rules, but it certainly is against theirs. Both schools have to think of their reputations. What you do and who you see in the holidays is your own business. But in termtime it is our business. This correspondence is forbidden. Do you understand?"

Penguins

You only need thirteen people to play 'house cricket'. This is for giving the better players a chance for some practice, as the batsmen are rotated with the fielders and the game goes on. But of course, the batsmen and bowlers are always the school team hopefuls, and the rest are just 'fielding fodder'. I was bored with all this, and after two years at the college I had the option of choosing another sport.

After some consideration I opted for sailing. The sailing boats were kept on the beach well down towards The Crumbles, a long way beyond the limit of College 'bounds' at Terminus Road. This liberty was peculiarly satisfying. No prefects, and no reproaches if you looked hopefully at girls. We sailed open twelve foot dinghies called Penguins; they were very similar in lines to National Twelves, except they lacked the latter's half-decking, which conveniently kept the sea out. Penguins were quite fast, but you couldn't risk leaning too far over as if the gunwhale went under the surface, the boat quickly filled with water and lay there waterlogged, and maybe overturned. But after learning how to rig and crew the little boat, I was finally allowed to helm it. There is no thrill like it - bouncing over the waves, hard on the wind, and balancing boat and crew alike while the waves and wind conspire to tip you into the drink. We always wore Admiralty cork lifejackets. These are clumsy things, but a sensible precaution when you are trying to right a capsized dinghy in the Channel on a May afternoon. I had no idea that water could be so cold!

Once a year the choir had a treat - a trip to sing with other school choirs in Canterbury Cathedral. I thought - I even knew - that we were pretty good. But there was a surprise in store. We revelled in the sound we made in that great towering nave, as nearly two hundred voices joined together, in praise possibly of God, but certainly of human musical genius. We really "made a joyful noise unto the Lord". And then the Cathedral Choir sang the same pieces. I think there were only twenty four of them. But the purity of their voices and the precision of their singing outshone us completely: it was like being exposed to the mathematics of singing - the naked soul of the music itself. So we were good: but we still had a long way to go!

It was on one of those Canterbury trips that John Dibb brought along a little ukelele, and entertained us to some Music Hall songs in the coach. I thought "how great to be able to bring your own music along, and get everyone singing". It was a very happy trip for me. And it seeded an ambition to do the same. I eventually became something of a minstrel myself in later years.

Summer

Dad seemed relaxed and happier than for ages. As soon as the cricket season started, he was off with the Waldron team every Saturday afternoon. When

they won they would repair to the Star in Waldron for a beer or two. And with every round, Simon, still the team's mascot, continued to get his half pint on the floor. Simon had a trick: when you were out walking at night, he loved being allowed to hold the old bicycle lamp between his teeth to light the way for you. One evening we heard the Ute return, and pull up in the yard. It was a dark night. Up the path came this strange faded pink light, weaving from side to side. And in came Simon, holding the torch backwards in his mouth, so it lit-up his cheeks from inside! When we took it from him, he seemed to be grinning foolishly: Dad was grinning too. So we knew it had been a good match.

Patrick Leaving for School

HMS Battleaxe

The Naval cadet 'camp' this summer was on a modern destroyer. She was very different from the Vanguard, being less than a quarter of the size, and she was a working warship, in full commission. There were fewer of us this year. Once again we used one of the Boy-Seamen's messes while they were on shore leave. We spent our days on practical sailing techniques. We learned to do bowlines with our eyes shut, and all the other routine knots with them open. This is a measure of the importance of bowlines in boatwork. We rowed in a heavy naval cutter, which is a thirty foot open boat used for transport between ships and the shore. And we sailed in the graceful twenty seven foot whalers, canoe sterned and beautiful. I got talking to one of the boy seamen while we were both showering after sailing. "Yeah, I'm grateful the Navy took me." "Oh, wouldn't you prefer to be at home sometimes?" "Nar. See, my Dad went off, and Mum couldn't keep me on track. I was always jumping school, and I got in with a bad lot. We was always breaking stuff, and we started nickin' stuff too. The Police suggested I joined up. I didn't have to. I think the Sergeant liked me. But I'm glad they took me, 'cos if they 'adn't, I'd a' bin in Borstal before long. The Navy's my home now." Rather different from the country solicitors sons who were my classmates.

The Heron Dinghy beside the Thames

Lockinge

Our previous visits to Robertsbridge had been replaced by holidays at Wantage in Berkshire, where my Uncle Alan (Tommy) and Aunt Margaret now lived. Uncle Tommy had given up the garage, and was now head of engineering and maintenance for a big agricultural company at the foot of the Berkshire Downs. He had about twenty tractors, including huge Caterpillar crawlers so big they needed a small diesel engine as a starter motor. There was a fleet of combine harvesters, and he did most of the maintenance himself with a team of mechanics in a big workshop at Lockinge, a small village belonging to the estate. Breakdowns during harvest time had to be repaired in the field, with five thousand acres of corn standing waiting. I watched him working to replace a cylinder-head gasket on an International combine in a field up near The Ridgeway. The wheels had sunk in the earth, deforming the runners which supported the engine. He put a jack under the engine to lift it up, and eased it back into place. I said I was surprised the chassis bent so easily. He replied "Agricultural machinery is made a bit flexible intentionally: if it can flex a little under stress, it is much less likely to break." He was a wise and patient engineer, with a deft touch for getting to the bottom of a problem quickly.

Nonie and I spent our holidays there cycling over the Downs, and along the chalk streams and past the watercress beds at their foot. A favourite expedition was out to Wantage Road station, on the Great Western main railway line to the West Country. To see an express thundering past at over one hundred miles an hour, drawn by one of the mighty Castle class steam locomotives, was to see and feel raw power in its most concentrated form. The rails shook and the air drummed for two miles each side of an express. At the other end of the scale, the station had a beautiful old tank engine dating from 1867, which used to draw the trains on the local steam tramway from Wantage town. The Shannon was lovingly restored when it finally retired from active service.

Shannon at Wantage Road Station

Uncle Tommy was a very trusting man. He had bought a lovely little sailing dinghy, a Heron, which he kept on the Thames just below the famous stone bridge at Abingdon. She was just slightly smaller than the Eastbourne Penguins, but with the advantage of a smart half-deck. When he heard I had taken up sailing, he took us to Abingdon one evening, showed Nonie and I how to set up the gunter rigged mainsail, and then simply let us get on with it. We had some happy afternoons sailing on Old Father Thames that summer.

Nonie with Pixie & Angela Simpson

Country Sports

With two ponies on the farm, Nonie and Penny were in their element. They shared a bedroom, and relations were often strained in termtime. But during the holidays they were the best of friends. Penny told me years later that they used to get up in the first light of dawn, and climb out of the house out of the stairs window and down over the pantry roof to the ground. Then they went out to the fields, caught Pixie - very willing - and Gunner - reluctant - and rode them bareback in the dewy grass using just their halters as reins, Indian style. "It was murderously hard on our backsides, particularly with Gunner's lumpy backbone, but it made us much better riders." They thought Mum and Dad knew nothing about it: I am not so sure, very little got past them. But Dad usually kept quiet about what he knew. They soon had a little Pony Club of a few friends: there was Anne Rayner, Gunner's owner and Nonie's classmate from Lewes; and little Angela Simpson from down the road. She was younger than everyone else, but she was an only child who had lived only with adults for much of her life, and hardly knew how to be young. Then there was Michelle Williams, a year older than Penny, who owned a beautiful little show pony called High Jinks, or usually just Jinks: small but handsome and very fast in gymkhanas. I tagged along to these events, which were often parallel to the Agricultural Shows. These were the big events for the farmers, with all the latest machinery on display, and judging of the show cattle and horses, and sometimes the fancy breeds of chickens too. There was a lot of thirst-quenching in the Harveys and Ind-Coope refreshment tents. Almost all the pony riders were girls, daughters of farmers and well-off country dwellers. I looked on hopefully. But their relationships with their animals left no room for human interests, as far as I could tell.

During that summer I sometimes also went to the Steeplechases, or Point-to-Points as they were known. Traditionally, hunts raced from the shadow of the steeple in one parish to that in the next one. These were the amateur level of true horse racing, where good hunters were raced against each other for cups and prize money, which would certainly help with defraying the considerable costs of keeping a horse. People accepted that the country enthusiasm for hunting was the price of the existence of this level of horse racing, with its colour and excitement; with the bookmakers and tickets, tipsters and touts, the viewing paddock before the race, the drumming of hooves and the flying mud of the last straight, and the splattered grinning triumph of the winners, the torn-up betting slips, and the consoling pat-down for the losers afterwards. I loved this world. But as far as real hunting was concerned, my sympathy was rather with the fox than the red-faced Colonel-types who hunted them. Young fox cubs play happily in the presence of humans in the fields; at that age they have no fear of us. Even though they kill chickens given the chance, foxes are a part of wild nature, completely independent of the human world. But there are spine-chilling overlaps. From Selwyns Wood in springtime there sometimes came long blood-curdling sobbing screams, like a child in mortal fear. We were told it was the cry of a vixen to her mate. I fervently hoped that was correct!

> With the steady success of the pullets being raised for meat,
> I decided in this spring to go back into breeding again. So
> I purchased some better quality chicks to raise as a new
> breeding stock. After growing out of the brooder house,
> these were put into free range pens in the fields. These had

been steam cleaned since their last use. But some chickens got out, and may have got into some old folds that were being broken up for firewood, being uneconomic to repair. In June the old symptoms re-appeared among these birds. It soon spread into the brooder house. As I had learned from past experience there was no way of avoiding Lewes, I determined to get this business settled once and for all. I wrote to the Divisional Officer, reporting the symptoms as my legal responsibility, and expressing the hope that if it was not fowl pest that they would help me to get to the bottom of the trouble. Mr Hunter came round: he appeared open-minded and seemed really anxious to help. He took some blood tests "to get rid of the possibility of fowl pest", and conceded that it was not unreasonable for me to feel that if it was not fowl pest, then some other disease was causing all these losses. The tests were presumably satisfactory, as the standstill order was soon lifted.

There were symptoms we had experienced before, such as a peculiar smell associated with the birds as opposed to their droppings. Mortality was not as high as I had expected, but the birds were showing a phenomenal thirst, standing in their drinking bowls and exhausting their day's supply before nine a.m. and fighting for more. I was at this time feeding home mixed mash, as considerable savings can be made in comparison with compounders feeds. The Ministry advisors felt that this was a weak point and concentrated their criticisms on this. One point after another was suggested as needing amendment. The investigation was obviously getting nowhere, and the losses were lower now, and as a planned break in production was coming up, to empty the farm of stock, I wrote to the D.O. to say that perhaps this time I had been mistaken.

I re-started with new stock in the brooder house in November '54, and these very quickly developed the same symptoms, slight colds and a respiratory 'rattle', and a much higher mortality than normal in the first fortnight. On starting to kill the Christmas chickens I found that losses had been far higher than I had expected from staff reports, and some weighed less than before they were put in the fattening pens. I called in the vets again. Hunter said that if he took blood tests he would be obliged to put the farm under a standstill order. As only dead stock were leaving the farm, he offered to leave us to benefit from the higher pre-Christmas prices. I was determined to make a supreme effort after the holiday to get the whole business cleared up.

Christmas 1954

Dad collected me from Eastbourne in the Ute. He was obviously worried, and questioned me closely about school work and exams. There had not been any except school end-of-term exams since O-Level. "You have to work very hard, both for the Navy exams and for A-Levels. Whatever happens, you cannot stay on at Eastbourne beyond the summer term, so this is your only chance". I knew that things had not gone well this year. But Dad did not discuss his financial problems. When we got back home the stock problems were obvious. The adult birds looked as if they had 'flu, and had weepy eyes and mucous filled nostrils. When they breathed there was a bubbly rattling sound in their throats. In the closed pens there was a nasty rancid sort of smell about them, like gone-off meat. We still had two workers at the farm, who took holidays over Christmas. Nonie and Penny and I helped with the feeding during the holiday season. Mother did her best, and the Christmas dinner was good. But it was not a light-hearted family this year that assembled round the dining room table. I had brought work home from Eastbourne for preparation of the exams. I was also writing a prize essay on the Use of Chemicals in Agriculture, as Chemistry was my best subject at school.

1955

Weybridge

Immediately after Christmas I collected blood samples from sick birds, and took them to the MoA laboratory in Weybridge with some specimen carcasses for examination. I told the Director that I was not satisfied with my treatment locally. Indeed it seemed to me that the only explanation of all the symptoms was fowl pest. If the farm was indeed infected and not cleaned out, it was most likely the primary cause of the continuing series of outbreaks in East Sussex. Shortly after this I was visited at the farm by Mr Black, the Superintending Veterinary Officer for the South East Region (Surrey, Kent, and Sussex). He sought to reassure me that Weybridge would get to the bottom of the trouble. But when I pointed out the original source of the infection in the neglect of Oakes birds back in 1950, he refused to listen at all.

Subsequently I had further contacts with the Weybridge vets, who were sympathetic but doubted that fowl pest could be the cause. They mentioned again the nervous symptoms, and I told them we had quite a few cases. The vet said that in cases of fowl pest the nervous symptoms were caused by brain inflammation: this could only be diagnosed if live cases were sent for examination, as sections of the brain have to be removed and prepared while still warm. I supplied more specimens. The PM reports found some traces of coccidiosis in the chicks, but one of the vets said there are no PM symptoms of fowl pest in young chicks. However, the report of the examination of the brains of nervous type specimens did in fact show inflammatory changes but "In the light of the circumstances of the case, we do not regard it of as much significance". What was special about 'the circumstances of the case' to make a positive finding of the symptoms they were testing for to be 'insignificant'?

On the advice of Weybridge I tried feeding the birds with the new antibiotic Terramycin. In the quantities they prescribed it had no apparent effect. So I sought the advice of the manufacturers. They recommended feeding a course for ten days at a very much higher dosage. The test flock improved greatly, appetites returned, and they gained weight rapidly. I put all new batches of growers on the drug treatment. However, after a few weeks the previous symptoms returned. Pfizer's representative said that once before they had to use two courses of treatment to get on top of an infection. So I repeated the treatment As soon as the treatment stopped the trouble flared up alarmingly. It rapidly became as bad as the acute outbreak in 1950 - 51. The mortality rose alarmingly, and it became impossible to keep the birds clean as they fouled the litter so rapidly with diarrhoea. I do not know whether the Terramycin had destroyed the infection in the chicks, and at the same time destroyed the immunity that the flock had built up. But it appeared that they were re-infected immediately, and this time they had no resistance.

Easter Holidays

Things were getting worse at the farm. The tractor had disappeared. No-one mentioned it. Now the feed was carried round the remaining adult birds in sacks on our backs. Of the workers only Dave Fenner remained. We all helped with the tasks of running the farm. Increasingly this meant picking up the carcases of the birds which had died, to be burned in the brooder-house boiler. Dad was looking gaunt, and seldom smiled. He never mentioned the financial situation of the farm, but obviously we were making very little money. The buildings were looking dilapidated. In an effort to present a more cheerful appearance to the world, I found a tin of white paint, and re-painted the main gate to the yard.

Burns

I was present one day when Mr Burns the vet came around on an inspection of the farm. Things looked very bad; anyone could see the stock were sick, with discharging eyes and nostrils, and birds lying dead in the runs and the brooder house. I was out of my depth, and kept quiet. Burns was a fiftyish man, with receding hair , a short gingery moustache, and a gruff Scots accent. For the whole visit he had been pointing out to my father why this disease could not be fowl pest (although every known symptom was there before him.) He emphasised that the blood test was very reliable, and he said it had never given a reaction.

Dad had picked up a carcase on the way, a poor looking thing about eight weeks old, just out of the brooder house. Burns agreed to examine it, and laid out his tools on the table of the incubator room in the oast house. He took his dissecting scissors, which had a small metal ball to blunt one point, made an incision below the neck, and cut along the length of the breast bone. "You see, Mr Brown, why this canna be fowl pest. Fowl pest has haemorrhages in the internal organs, sometimes in bad cases even in the verra bones themselves". He peeled back the flesh from the little runt's breastbone. A black and scarlet stain spread across half of it. My father pointed at the body. "Like that, you mean?" His voice was husky with suppressed emotion. Burns glanced up at him, then at me. Silently, he peeled back the flesh on the other side: the whole bone, from the neck to the wing root and thigh, was one huge bloodstain. Without a word he closed the carcase, packed up his tools, and walked out of the gate to his car. Then something else transpired. Another man had been waiting in the car, without entering the farm. He got out, and suddenly a furious row broke out between the two men. "That's Black", Dad said; "he's the supervisor of the whole South East of England". They looked across at us, then walked about fifty yards away down the road to the end of our Longshed, so that we couldn't hear what they were saying. But the gestures made it fairly obvious: Burns was enraged, and waving his arms about, shouting. Black seemed to be trying to pacify him. Eventually they walked back to the car, Burns with his face set in a fixed scowl. They neither said a word to us, Black did not even acknowledge our presence. They got into the car, and drove away. We never saw Burns again at the farm.

The Last Term

Although it was the occasion for the big exams, A-Level and the Navy Exams, it was a relief to be back in Wargrave. I had come to terms with life at the College, and was a Sixth Former myself now. Home was becoming a place I barely recognised. It was still my house, my family, my parents. But the sense of paralysing frustration over the whole place made it almost foreign to me. The stock were being destroyed by a disease which had every symptom of fowl pest, a legally notifiable disease. But for some incredible reason the Ministry vets, who were the only ones who could handle the disease, refused to admit that it was so. The birds were left to suffer and die, and we had no clean-up and no compensation. I realised by now that we were heading for ruin if the cycle of denial was not broken, but what could I do?

I turned to the exams. I was confident enough about Physics and Chemistry, as I was in the A sets with the best teachers in the school, 'Pinup' Perrens and Tommy Rodd respectively. I was in the B set for maths, but I was taking the joint exam called Pure and Applied Mathematics, which was an easier option. I had a seriously weak spot, as I had missed co-ordinate algebra in the wasted fifth form term, and I never really understood it. Instead of getting to the bottom of it, I tried remembering all the equations instead of the methods to derive them. It was not a good approach.

While preparing for the A-Level practicals I was rushing to do a volumetric analysis, and needing a measuring cylinder urgently: there was none to be had. Then I saw one, standing on the sill of an open window. It was nearly full of clear liquid. Supposing it to be water I was just about to tip it down the sink, when I thought I had better check, and stuck my nose in to have a sniff. My head seemed to nearly blow off: my eyes streamed with tears, I was choking, my nose went numb, and I couldn't see anything. When my eyes cleared several minutes later, the first thing I did was to look in a mirror to convince myself that my nose was still there. The reason for the open window became apparent - the clear liquid was .880 ammonia, the strongest concentration it is possible to make!

I cannot remember any written Navy exams; I think the College sent my O-Level results, and a prediction of my expected A-Level results. As a result I was invited to a one day interview and initiative test board in London. It was very similar to the 'command over an obstacle' type of test at Dartmouth, and there was another medical examination. This time they did not give the results on the spot, saying they would take about two months. Then came the concentrated silence over the school, as A-Levels started. In the sciences, the practical examinations came first. We had a qualitative analysis of some unknown chemical to perform. This was a feat of memory, as there is a six stage sequence of operations, each stage of which reduces the number of possible candidates for the base (usually a metal) of the compound, until you are down to one or two. Final distinction sometimes requires a flame test, where you dip a platinum wire into a solution of the stuff, and identify it from the colour of the flame. Then we had to identify the salt, or acid part of the compound. We had three hours to perform this, together with a measurement of concentration for another mystery substance. We had been well drilled, and we beavered away silently for a whole afternoon. Likewise for the physics practicals. Then the written exams came and went in intense concentration. By comparing with the other candidates we pretty soon found the correct answers afterwards, and I felt fairly confident of success. The Maths however was less certain: I hoped I had passed, but I wasn't sure.

Three weeks before the end of term, it was over for us, and the turn of the O-Level candidates. I was of course a 'leaver', but unlike many I was not heading for a University, as I was a candidate still for the Navy. Quite a number of my classmates were staying on for a senior year; to be prefects, or to take the Oxbridge scholarship exams in the autumn, or simply to play in the sports teams. But I was like a train coming out of a four year tunnel of school, not knowing what the open landscape of the future held. I passed the time doing a chemical analysis of a half gallon jug of seawater, which I steadily boiled away to concentrate the solution. I think I identified almost every chemical base in the book in the Channel seawater.

Frank Baker, of School House, was one of my classmates. He was one of these relaxed self confident people, never at loss for an answer. I suppose it was in the genes: we didn't know it, but his father was Air Chief Marshall Sir Frank Baker. He was an arch proponent of the languid catch-phrase - almost a sigh - "need I say more?" He was also secretary of the Sailing Club, my refuge. I will always remember his report on the Cloisters notice board of a three-way sailing match off the Crumbles:

Ardingly: retired,

Tonbridge: sank,

n.i.s.m ?

It was one of the last sporting events of my school career.

Leaving Day

The last day of term arrived. My feelings were very mixed. Eastbourne had been a sort of home for two thirds of the four years I was there. But they were far from 'the happiest years of my life'. In the tradition of the famous Arnold of Rugby, physical sports and team games were the only currency of any great value in school society. Academic success, at least for Oxbridge entrances, counted with the teachers at the end of your school career. But as far as the boys were concerned, that simply rated you as a 'swot' - which was acceptable if you were a sportsman on the field, but not otherwise. Music, like the minor sports except for rowing, rated nowhere. Only success on stage gained you any credit, as a good performance there was very visible to everyone. There was no violence, or any real bullying, at least in Wargrave. Disciplinary beatings were routine, but seldom unjust. If you broke the rules, you knew the likely price in advance, so there was no use complaining. What had spoiled the college experience for me was the whole student atmosphere; the sneering at virtually anything that did not conform to the Arnoldian expectation of *mens sane in corpore sana:* fit team players, sexually repressed, and no more intelligent than necessary to keep good discipline. But nevertheless, I had been through the mill, it had shaped me, and became part of me. I took my place in the choirstalls for the last time. Eastbourne, unlike parish church congregations, had a long tradition of singing out fully. The last service always triggered an emotional nerve; four hundred and thirty voices gave it everything they had. "Through all the changing scenes of life", then the School Psalm 121, "I will lift up mine eyes unto the hills, from whence cometh my help", shook the rafters while eyes welled up with blinked-back tears. We walked down the aisle and out into the uncertain sunlight of an English summer day. I shook hands with a few of the masters outside. "What will you do now?". "Where are you headed next?". Eastbourne had implanted the idea that I could not go to University without Latin, so the thought of using my evident enjoyment and facility with the Sciences simply had not occurred to me. I was still hoping for the Navy, but with less certainty than before. Other than that, I really had no idea.

Dad drove me home in the Ute, with my trunk and chattels, for the last time. At Willingdon Hill the Long Man watched me go, as blankly as he had watched me arrive under the Downs four years earlier. Dad did not say very much. I realise now, as I didn't at the time, that this was the end of a commitment he had made, and which he could not really afford even at the beginning, that I would have everything he had enjoyed in the way of education. Mother questioned me closely about my exam prospects; did I still want the Navy? Still living in my blinkers, I said yes. "Well, whatever happens, you will have to pay your own way. You are almost eighteen now, and we simply don't have enough money to keep supporting you. Which means you will have to find a job in the short term, at least to cover your costs. Things are not going very well."

For me, they soon got worse. A buff envelope On Her Majesty's Service arrived. I opened it : inside were two folded foolscap sheets, headed Royal Navy Spring Entrance Results. No personal letter then. I scanned the list: the top thirty or so came under the heading Passed. I could not find my name there. I re-read it. Then I looked further down, under Not Accepted : about fifteen lines down a list of two hundred was my name. After a few seconds it sank in. I felt giddy, and nearly lost my balance. I walked blindly out of the house and up the road a little way. My throat ached. My thought processes stopped; there was only this numb feeling spreading up from my stomach till it formed an acid bile in my throat, and the realisation clarified in my mind. I had failed. I had let my parents down. I had let myself down. All I had thought I wanted since boyhood was to join the Navy, and they had rejected me. Again. The landscape of my future life had vanished completely. Nobody said anything. It was obvious what had happened.

The Long Man of Wilmington

June 1955

The press reported a new outbreak of fowl pest at Haslemere in Surrey. I had sometime previously sold some live pullets in Guildford Market. This was an unusual outlet for me; it was an experiment as Smithfield prices for dead birds had been low at the time. As the first batches on the farm to go down so badly later this summer had been from the same age group, I wondered if the ones I had sold were the cause of the outbreak. So I wrote to the Superintending V.O. (Mr Black), telling him of my experience, and begging him to take the matter seriously. A few days later Vet Hunter came round and viewed the birds: they were a terrible sight, with mucous dripping from their eyes and bubbles forming on their nostrils, gasping, heeling over and choking to death in front of him. He took some blood samples, but made no comment at all. I was simply amazed that any responsible V.O. could see that sight and make no comment of any kind. I told him of the heavy losses, over one hundred birds weekly were dying. A few days later I was phoned from Lewes, and told the samples were alright, and I was free to move the birds if I wished. I could hardly believe it was possible.

I was wholly convinced by now that the disease had always been and could only be fowl pest; and that the Ministry vets, for some reason I could not fathom, were determined at all costs that this disease would never be diagnosed by them on my premises. I thought of a possible loophole. I carefully selected six live birds, all of which were showing obvious respiratory symptoms, and took them to a small Ministry-controlled laboratory at Wye in the neighbouring county of Kent, where I was unknown. Immediately I got inside with the crate of birds, which were coughing audibly, The Ministry vet , a Mr de Tillot, said "Where do you come from? Those birds look like fowl pest." I stated that I was having a lot of trouble and losses, and that "A pal of mine had suggested it might be 'Blue Comb'." In fact the Lewes vet had very half-heartedly put this idea forward. The Wye man scoffed at this. He questioned me closely about conditions on the farm, and I replied honestly, stating the losses without any reference to previous inquiries. Mr de Tillot said everything pointed to fowl pest as being the cause, and he further reproved me for moving the birds off the farm and into Kent. When he said Lewes would have to be notified at once, I asked if the whole thing could not be handled from Wye? But he was adamant on this, and I left. At least I felt fully restored to sanity, even if nothing else had been achieved. It confirmed that when the symptoms were given the unprejudiced consideration by an impartial man who should have been fully qualified to express an opinion, his diagnosis expressed in ordinary English coincided with mine. On returning home I was visited by a Police Patrol, who served a standstill order on me at 9.30 pm.

The following day Mr Hunter came from Lewes, demanding to know what I had said to the Wye man to make him believe that the farm had got fowl pest? I said I had put no ideas of my own to him, but that the specimens I took were obviously typical of fowl pest. Hunter said the Ministry wanted blood samples from the laying birds, which I had told de Tillot had dropped in production since Hunter's last visit. I was utterly disgusted by this attempt to avoid the main issue, which was the mounting losses of table poultry that he had chosen to completely ignore. I told him that the taking of blood samples at my farm was and always had been a farce, and that I was sure that his Lewes office had never treated me fairly or looked at the losses realistically. I forced him to look at the table birds, and pointed out the terrible condition of many of them, the coughing and gasping - which he said lamely that he had not noticed before. I told him further that the Lewes office had at no time put forward any worthwhile suggestion to account for my losses; and that having made my living here for over twenty years I did not require advice at the very elementary level on which they were trying to treat the whole matter. Next day he returned, saying the Ministry insisted on more tests: he took them and left.

When the police had served the standstill order on me, I noticed that it was Form B and not the usual Form A. Under Form B I was allowed to move dead birds. Believing that the Wye vet would have the courage of his convictions, I took a further six dead specimens, five of which had marked respiratory symptoms, to Wye. Mr de Tillot was out, so I left them for a post mortem. While I was away doing this the police came to the farm to change the order to Form A, saying the first order was in error.

I was then phoned by the Lewes office, and an appointment was made to meet Captain Elvin the Divisional (E.Sussex) Veterinary Officer. When he came with Mr Hunter he spoke at length about veterinary etiquette, and was most indignant that I should have gone to Wye without informing him. He was even more so when I told him that I had done it to obtain the spontaneous reaction of a qualified man who was not clearly prejudiced against me. He then asked several questions, all leading up to "What excuse had I to offer for moving birds while I was under a standstill order?" It was clear to me by then that the real reason for the visit was to prepare the way for court proceedings against me. I told him that at the time I was under a form B standstill order, and that my actions had been within the letter of the law. He was clearly disconcerted by this. However he offered to send once again an advisory officer to get to the bottom of the trouble; although he remarked that "I was putting some strain on the Ministry's time"!

I asked for a copy of de Tillot's report. Captain Elvin undertook to arrange this.

Later a report was received from Wye, which in cold detail was very critical of the farm, the management, the feeding, the lack of care, the careless caponising, and also starvation. (I had carefully chosen sick birds, and sick birds eat little or nothing.) It also made a completely untrue statement, saying only one of the birds showed respiratory symptoms - they almost all had them. My first reaction was that the whole thing was ridiculous, coming from a man who had never seen the farm at first hand , or been informed in detail of the management policy. I decided to ignore it. Later I felt uneasy, and then as the full possibilities dawned on me I felt downright scared. The use of the word starvation woke memories of Mr Oakes' experience. All the ingredients of another Cruelty to Poultry prosecution existed on my farm. Everything said of his birds could have been said of mine, and with plenty of Ministry vets to give evidence I would not have an earthly chance.

A Cross-Country Drive

Dad asked if I would like to come on a trip to Wye? I was still rather numb from being turned down by the Navy, and having no clear idea what I wanted to do now. So a trip made a break at least. I knew that Dad had made two visits there in recent weeks; and that he had high hopes at first, but that they had been dashed. Dad had prepared one of the best table birds, plucked, dressed, and carefully packed in a farm labelled box. I asked what was the point? "de Tillot told me at first that the birds were showing every symptom of fowl pest. Then evidently he was leaned on, either by Lewes or somebody further up the line. So he sent a critical report, blaming the farm management for all the trouble, saying it was down to careless - possibly criminal - farming. The vets themselves have said there is no really conclusive PM test for fowl pest. So what they see, they can ignore, or blame on other causes. I took a dozen birds with advanced respiratory disease; it was not even mentioned in the report! So I am taking this perfect bird, to show him that a farm which can produce such stock is not mismanaged at all." "It seems a long shot to me." "Well then, think of it as irony if you like. But we are desperate. We are running out of stock, and money, and I can't think of any way out. Can you?" So we drove across the Weald into Kent in the gentle summer evening sunlight. At Wye the laboratory was shut for the day. Dad left the packet, carefully addressed to de Tillot, with the watchman, who promised to deliver it. We drove back again into the oncoming night. Overhead a low flying fighter plane was heading slowly in the same direction. It was a delta winged Javelin, produced as part of Duncan Sandys' determination to keep the RAF able to stand off the Russian menace at the coldest point of the Cold War. "Do you find it comforting that they are up there, looking after our interests?", I asked. "No", he replied. "I would have, once. But now I don't trust the Civil Service or the military to look after anyone's interest but their own". My father's view of the behaviour of officialdom, when private interest collided with public duty, was understandably pretty sour. We drove home with little more to say.

Two days later the chicken was returned by post, with a letter saying de Tillot declined to accept it in the circumstances. Either he could not appreciate counter-evidence, or somebody had leaned on him so hard that he dared not recognise it.

Careers

At Dad's suggestion I phoned Eastbourne to see if anyone was at the careers advice office. 'Goofy' Godden was in. So I went down to see him. "Well, what have we got for scientists? Let me see. Since you like the sea, you could join the Merchant Marine; maybe as a Radio Officer. Should be worth about £2000 a year by the time you are thirty. Or how about engineering? You should ideally have the two Maths A-Levels, but maybe the joint one would do." He gave me the recruitment pamphlets for Rolls-Royce, Bristol Aircraft, and EMI. I applied to Rolls, and went up to Derby for an interview, staying for a couple of days with Eric and Gladys on top of the hill at Milford again. The interview with one of the engineers went reasonably well. He said "If you get an engineering apprenticeship with us, we will send you for a degree, spread over four years, and give you practical training too. But be aware you will have to work very hard. There is no magic recipe for being Rolls-Royce - we simply work much harder than any other company." I noticed his rather attractive secretary looking at me speculatively, and I thought "Well, there are certainly worse places than here to start a career." My A-Level results arrived. As expected, I passed both Physics and Chemistry. And, as feared, I had failed Pure and Applied Maths. I wrote to Rolls, asking if they would take me on, and let me sit a re-take on Maths: they replied saying apply again when I had got it. It looked as if there were few careers available without the third pass.

Meanwhile I needed to get some money coming in. Mother had heard that Mrs Postlethwaite had regular part-time jobs, so I went to see her down Moat Lane. She ran the catering stands at Brands Hatch motor racecourse. So for much of the summer and autumn I was there at weekends, working behind the bars selling coffee, or carrying around a sandwich tray on a neck strap. I got £2 10s per day, and gave half to mother. It helped anyway. I also saw the rise to glory of Jack Brabham, and the unstoppable success of the racing D-Type Jaguars, which were the base for the unforgettable E-type, still one of the world's most desirable cars.

August 1955. Advice

Feeling by now thoroughly roused, I took all my troubles
to an old friend of my wife's family, Mr Norman Gingell
JP, who was chairman of Hertfordshire County Council
and a qualified bacteriologist, with a wealth of farming
knowledge and experience of administration. He came down
to the farm to see us, looked around, and was immediately
struck by the short distances separating the half dozen
small farms involved in this story. Coming from a county of
much larger farms, it struck him immediately that a single
farm of a thousand acres could have contained all of the
infected farms here. He expressed the opinion that under the
circumstances the infection could only be fowl pest; and that
"It was not a question of something being wrong with the
Ministry Vets treatment of me, but rather there was nothing
right about it". He advised me to write down all the facts
in detail, and send them off at once to my MP. This I did.
Unfortunately at that time I did not have certain information,
which came my way later. I posted the letter on the 6th of
September, to my MP Mr Godman Irvine, member for the
Rye constituency of East Sussex. It was briefly acknowledged.

Conditions on the farm became extremely bad. In spite of the high mortality we
still had a large flock of poultry. We went round the chicken runs in the morning
and evening, collecting the casualties. You pick up a dead hen by its feet. But it
was a hot July and August: chicken that die of fowl pest, a virus disease which
produces a high fever, decompose amazingly quickly. We had to be very careful
lifting a carcase by the feet, as after a few hours, the legs would pull straight out
of the body. The stench of rancid meat was foul. The bodies were incinerated - ten
to fifteen each day. The chicken were not finishing all of their rations of mash,
put out twice daily in their feeding troughs. But others were helping themselves.
Wild birds, seeing the untouched food, started feeding at the troughs. Rooks and
crows, being carrion eaters, also started to tear apart the corpses of dead chickens
as they lay there. What happened was inevitable: the disease broke out among the
wild birds too. I found a poor blackbird, fluttering vainly against the wire netting,
trying weakly to escape from a hen-run. I caught it in my hands. How many
people do you know who have caught a wild bird in their hands? I looked at it. Its
yellow bill was streaked with mucous, and its eyes were almost blocked with pus -
the poor thing was nearly blind. I set it down: half an hour later it was dead. Next
day I found a rook, expiring in a corner of a run. It was very distressed, choking
and 'rattling' in its throat, just like the chickens. It threatened me defiantly with

its beak, so I did not touch it. Dad sent the corpse to Weybridge laboratory for PM. The result came back "Severe respiratory symptoms and inflammation".

With the wild birds of the woods and hedges now dying helplessly, what chance did we, or the other farms around, now have?

The Unbelievable Clue

I had some information about this time from a journalist in Brighton, who had tried to help me. He interviewed Captain Elvin, the District VO in East Sussex, asking about the situation of fowl pest in the County. He asked him successively about the symptoms by which the disease could be recognised. Then he asked "Then why, Captain Elvin, do you not diagnose the disease when all the symptoms are present among the birds at Mr Armstrong Brown's farm at Cross-in-Hand?" Captain Elvin replied "That diagnosis was carried out on the orders of my superior". At the time I was told this I could not believe it, thinking as I did then that the prejudice against me existed at the level of the Lewes County Office.

Brighton Pavilion

Autumn 55

Mr Godden had said that I could possibly go to a Technical College to do further study, and get extra A-Levels if necessary. So I went down to Brighton Tech, and got the necessary forms. This was a completely different world. The College Calender laid out many parallel paths to complete careers: not only the pure sciences, but also electrical mechanical and civil engineering, electronics, pharmacy, economics, catering, domestic science, surveyors and accountants; it seemed as if they had everything. You could study by day for London University External Degrees, or in the evenings for Ordinary and Higher National Diplomas, as well as professional society Diplomas. Dad said that the fees of £26 for two terms would be affordable. I signed–up for the one year Intermediate X course to retake Maths, this time as two Subjects.

On the 24th of September fowl pest was confirmed at Green Vale Farm, some 500 yards away, and the stock was slaughtered. From conversations I later learned that the vets had been investigating the case for two weeks before making up their minds. This would have coincided with the time when my story was put before Mr Nugent, at that time the Under Secretary for Agriculture. He was a well known and experienced poultry breeder himself; so he should have been perfectly well aware of the legal requirements and the full implications from the angle of the Poultry Industry. No doubt exists in my mind that with the long history of the disease in the district, particularly at Woodbine Farm and several others, he must have felt that the Animal Health Division of the Ministry had failed lamentably. So it was probably on his orders that no less than five vets attended that small outbreak. I was visited by a West Sussex vet, who said that he and a man from Kent had been sent in to help out the East Sussex vets (or more likely to see that they did their job properly.) He inspected our farm, and took blood samples, remarking that the blood was clearly not normal, and that many birds were sick. He placed the farm under a form B standstill order, which was maintained for a month. But although weeks passed, I heard nothing from Mr Nugent, nor had any investigation on the farm.

So for the first time I joined the Lewes school students waiting for the 18 bus at Cross-in-Hand in the mornings. I had applied to the County for a student bus season ticket, which was granted. I was amazed, and delighted, at how friendly everyone was, both on the bus and at Brighton. There was none of the atmosphere of belittling of others, which was endemic at Eastbourne College. Instead, friendship was available and open, and hilarious conversations about anything and everything were the common currency. The high point of the week was The Goon Show on the BBC Radio, and we all hurried home to enjoy it. Next day on the bus the previous evening's programme would be recounted and quoted, and the irreverent approach to life became our understanding of the world. It was zany, but it was entirely healthy in its reaction to the rather stuffy 'Britishness' of our schooling. Even our Mother joined in to hear the show with us, taking a little while to identify Neddy Seagoon, and Peter Sellers' four or five alter-egos, and with the weekly humiliation of the stalwart BBC man John Snagge. I think the Goons helped to keep us sane that autumn.

From a letter to Dr Blount; BOCM Poultry Advisory Service. My wild bird experiences would, I'm sure, have interested you. (Your letter says).. that there is little evidence of natural infection. .....I should say that there has been considerable evidence of this with the smaller birds - blackbirds, thrushes, chaffinches and yellowhammers have all been observed, some with both nervous and respiratory symptoms. Several dead rooks were taken from the cattle troughs.... The sight of a rook, perched on the side of a trough and plunging it's head right down in the water, exactly as I have seen many chickens do when the fever is at it's height, made me aware of the significance of this. Later a young jackdaw was caught, showing nervous symptoms, partially paralysed and sitting back on its tail, as I had seen many chicken do in the last stages. It was sent alive to Weybridge laboratory. They were trying to keep it alive, as it seemed tame and in otherwise good condition. It died unexpectedly. On examination, they could find no reason for the paralysis of the leg.

Yellowhammer

As a youth of not quite eighteen, coming from a country home and a repressive schooling, Brighton Tec was a real culture shock. Young men and some very attractive girls mingled all around perfectly naturally. I didn't know at first how to talk to the girls. At lunchtimes there was the fascinating institution of the 'Penny Hop'. This was an hour long dance session most lunchtimes. The pennies bought new records when they wore out. The dancing was mostly ballroom dancing, which I had learned years before - except for exotic dances like tangos, and the proper way to do the foxtrot. Here as elsewhere in those days, the girls hoped to find a boy who could dance properly. They wanted a partner who could lead them confidently through the steps they knew, twirl them so their skirts flared out, and generally make them look and feel good. A boy's looks were not everything by any means! Then there was a dance called Jive, which was done to Jazz. The cool customers managed to Jive while smoking, partnering the whirling girls with one hand while holding a burning fag in the other. As I stood on the edge of this melee, screwing up my courage; the issue was suddenly resolved when a friendly girl from Intermediate Pharmacy simply invited me! I coped, and suddenly found both my feet and my tongue. I entered a whole new social world.

Brighton Tec was somehow a cross between a senior school for teaching, and a University for the student life on offer. The 'lectures', as they were called , were mostly informal classes in normal classrooms. The lecturers treated us as adults, and because the classes were fairly small we could always get a question or a difficulty treated on the spot. We became friends with most of them in the first few weeks. I kept my hand in by also taking the Physics course, and this was to be my salvation. But I was really there for the Maths. And in that I received my greatest stroke of luck, as my Mathematics lecturer was Richard Goodman. He was one of the only two authentic geniuses I have ever known personally - the other was a Nobel prizewinner. Not only was Mr Goodman a mathematical genius, he was also a brilliant teacher who could make difficult subjects completely transparent, and thus appear simple. By the end of my first week in his course, all my difficulties with coordinate algebra had vanished. Now I really understood the method behind the subject. Once that was clear, the particular topics could easily be derived, and their problems solved systematically. I advanced further in a week with him than I had at Eastbourne in a year. He was a slightly stooped man with a thick shock of greying hair, smiling but intent eyes, and a prominent hawk-like nose. He was reputed to be a communist in private; and he would sometimes divert us with humorous mini-lectures on economics, using such examples as the 'witchety-grub economy' of the Australian Aborigines. But whatever his real convictions were, he kept them out of the lectures. However, we did once meet the other staff of the physics department looking shaken and a bit pale: it seems they had just attended a staff training lecture Mr Goodman had given on matrix and tensor mathematics. The subject would shake anyone!

On the fourth of November a reply was received from the Ministry of Agriculture. Mr Nugent appeared to have referred the whole matter to the vets and accepted any explanation that they cared to make, and without any examination of the farm by an impartial advisor he virtually dismissed the matter. He referred to various deficiencies and shortcomings mentioned at different times, and said that if attention was paid to these he felt sure that results would improve. I replied at once that all the suggestions had been acted upon, sometimes with the most disastrous consequences, and no improvement had resulted. Further, that when outside birds bought for breeding had been mixed with my stock they had caught the disease immediately, which removed the question of so-called deficiencies, even if the death of large numbers of birds had not already done so.
The Ministry replied that, in the

Robin on the Gatepost

circumstances, a visit by the Superintending Vet, Mr Black, seemed the best way of dealing with the matter. When he arrived, he said he could well understand that I suspected fowl pest in view of all the symptoms. (This was an interesting reversal, in view of the Lewes vets long attempt to bluff!) But he said he could not understand why no reaction to the blood test had occurred.

I now know that there is in fact no statutory requirement for the blood test, called the Haemagglutination Inhibition Test, in diagnosis of Newcastle Disease, commonly called fowl pest. Therefore if all the other symptoms are present, nothing prevents the vets from confirming the disease, except for other reasons beyond diagnostic requirements. After a long wait, with the farm almost continuously under a standstill order, to say that I was disappointed with this brush-off would understate my mental state by a long way.

I had scraped together a few pounds from my Brands Hatch earnings. I had also learned where in Brighton the students could eat very cheaply at lunchtime. For one choice they could go to the students canteen up on the hill towards Kemptown. But it was crowded and noisy, and you could eat better near the college at the Place Pigalle (the pig 'ole!), or in the basement of the Tudor Hotel in the Old Steyne. It was here that I first saw someone actually playing an antique Spanish guitar. She was a tall unkempt hippy from the Art College next door. The instrument fascinated me. I added some money Gran had given me for my birthday with the rest of my small savings, and I bought my first guitar for £7 10s, together with a book of basic instructions. By great good luck it introduced me to true 'finger-style' playing. Soon I was back at the basement of the Tudor Hotel, learning tunes and picking up songs. My photographic memory for music that interested me made me a quick learner.

> Writing to the Superintending Vet Mr Black later, as I
> thought at the time he was genuinely anxious to help, I
> asked if it was not strange that, at the beginning of all
> this history, the vet tracing contacts from a confirmed
> infection (Selwyns Farm) to another farm, (Mr Oakes),
> where many poultry were found dead, had taken no further
> action? Mr Black replied very curtly, saying he had nothing
> further to add to his previous remarks; that no reaction
> had occurred among the large number of blood tests taken,
> and that therefore fowl pest could not have been the cause
> of my losses. It seems likely that from the end of August
> until December, the Ministry policy had been to keep my
> farm almost continuously under a standstill order, so
> as to ensure the rundown of the stock and my complete
> ruin. If that was not their intention, it was certainly
> their effect - as they must have known it would be.

A Career Possibility?

The Intermediate Physics course was given by Dr Niel Pentland. Among all our friendly lecturers, he alone had the teaching style and attitudes of a very straight schoolmaster. A very formal man, always wearing a dark business suit, with a balding head and florid complexion, he nevertheless introduced me to new perceptions in physics, even if I already had the A-Level. As head of the Physics Department, he was trying to open up a new 'Sandwich Course', which would lead to a college diploma in Applied Physics. He already had offers from companies such as Mullard, and others such as the Ministry of Supply, to give students job experience, and even staff positions, while they were training. The details were still unclear, as Sandwich Courses were a totally new departure; but the field of applying physics to instrument and engineering problems in a practical way sounded fascinating, and the prospect of a salary while still studying sounded too good to be true. It was certainly worth hanging on for.

1956

February

Having been brought face to face with bankruptcy, I finally found the missing link in the chain of events when talking to my neighbour Mr McCredie at Galingale. I mentioned the name of Mr Black in the conversation. He exclaimed, "Why, that's the man!" "Which man?" "That is the name of the vet who did the diagnosis at Selwyns farm, back at the beginning, when Miss Gamman's stock was killed out. He was the District Vet for East Sussex at the time. Then Hunter took over at Oakes' farm."

Suddenly the whole story made sense! Although only last summer I could not believe it, it was clear now that when Captain Elvin said that the diagnosis of my farm was made on his superior's orders, he must have been speaking the literal truth. Black had failed in his legal obligation to inspect a close contact of the confirmed case at Selwyns Farm, namely Mr Oakes at Hilden Farm. As a result the farmer had been wrongly prosecuted for cruelty to poultry, with the Ministry Vets standing complacently by. Oakes' birds infected mine, and mine and his caused confirmed infections via the Heathfield market. Oakes sold up and left the county in disgrace. Sometime around 1950 Black was promoted to Regional Superintendent for the South East. Only I, unaware of any of this, remained stubbornly and desperately in business. The continuing infection at my farm was living evidence firstly of the initial carelessness, then later of successive layers of cover-up and abuse of authority.

Woody Nightshade

While he was the responsible vet at county level, one man had the authority to suppress the diagnosis at Oakes, and later at our farm. In context it makes sense that Hunter, and Burns, then later MacDonald, were initially sure that they were dealing with fowl pest; that is until they took their story back to Lewes. Hunter and Burns came back changed in demeanor, denying that the disease could possibly be fowl pest, having perhaps been suborned by someone in a senior position; someone with a reason to deny that a mistake was made, and with the authority to make the denial stick. Maybe someone who was going for promotion? Maybe someone who, when he got promotion, was in a position to deflect the no doubt genuine requests from Ministry headquarters for an investigation, prompted via the NFU in 1952 and by Godman Irvine MP in 1955. Although requested twice from the Ministry, no inspection took place on the farm. Who got in the way? In spite of pressure, Burns rebelled after the bone haemorrhages were found in front of witnesses, and he was never seen again at the farm. Likewise the sympathetic MacDonald and the West Sussex vet were moved away. de Tillot was initially so sure that our live birds had fowl pest that he had a standstill order served in a neighbouring county. His later retraction, and his condemnation of a farm he had never seen, looked like the reaction of a man under pressure. Who was his hierarchical superior? Who had much to lose if the affair was ever brought to light? One man. The man my father had trusted.

By now the whole family knew some of the situation. The debts of the farm exceeded the assets available to cover them. Our creditors had a meeting: Dad returned, silent, and looking somehow shrunken. Mother told us later that the creditors refrained from pushing for bankruptcy proceedings, as there was little prospect of even the Bank recovering its money, and there would be none for the others. The only hope that they had of seeing our debts repaid was for Dad to prove his case in an action against the Ministry. The meeting approved his proposal to apply for Legal Aid to pursue the case.

Nonie was sixteen at this time: she knew at least as much as me of the situation, as she had been at the farm the whole time, and our mother confided in her a lot. Penny was thirteen, and while by nature an optimist, she certainly understood that the situation was serious. Patrick was nine. As the youngest, I think everyone naturally tried to shield him from the reality. But he could see it with his own eyes. The fact that nobody explained what was going on probably made things worse for him as, contrary to our good intentions, it only made him feel more isolated.

The Night Ride

Popular songs in the nineteen fifties were mainly about two themes; there were either songs about Love, or ballads about Cowboys. Sometimes you had cowboys in love, as in The Streets of Laredo! Any young person was awash in endless ballads about love. And as I was becoming a minstrel, playing my small stock of songs on the bus or on the beach, I wanted some for myself. But the place for romance was the dancehall, dances were in the evenings, and I lived sixteen miles out into the countryside. The last bus home left Brighton at nine thirty in the evening. So, as spring slowly warmed the air and a young man's fancy, I decided on desperate measures. One morning I cycled all the way to Brighton, and chained my bike to a railing all day. In the evening I went up to the Tec main hall for the dance; the girl I intended to dance with - didn't turn up! Still, I danced well enough, but romance didn't come calling. At twelve o'clock I reluctantly unchained my bike, and set out for home. Nearly an hour later, and feeling saddle-sore, I knocked on the door of a pub whose light was still lit in Eastgate Street in Lewes, and asked if I could buy a long cool drink? Then I set out again, and slowly the miles wound beneath the wheels; Ringmer, the Broyle (an old Roman road), Halland, Bloody Hill, then uphill through Blackboys. As I came to Possingworth Park I noticed a faint but strengthening line of yellowish sky along the eastern horizon under a night-dark edge of cloud: it crept just around the tree trunks without lighting the branches. As I paused to look - I had no idea that dawn started this early - I heard a most beautiful sound. A bird close by was singing a liquid fluting sort of wild melody; after a minute it was answered by another further away. Then another and another, further distant yet, until the wood was ringing with their song. Nightingales! I knew of them, but I had never heard one before. I was weary enough to drop: but as I pedalled the final mile home, my heart was singing with the birds.

Home Sweet Home

The atmosphere at home was stomach-wrenchingly tense. I loved my home, my parents, and my family. But coming home in those days made me feel almost ill, with the sickening feeling of doom in the forefront of everyone's mind.

One day there was an envelope with the Eastbourne College crest lying on the desk. Wondering why they would be writing now about me, I glanced at

Penny and Nonie

the letter, and froze. It said that if my final term's fees remained unpaid, they would be obliged to take my father to court. I should not have looked - it was not addressed to me. Dad was trying to protect us from this. He was taking all the strain on himself, and was looking increasingly gaunt. And then thinking back, I realised with a sinking feeling why the tractor had vanished last Easter: he had sold it to pay my penultimate term school fees.

Things were disappearing around the house: one day I noticed that a lovely carved ivory chess set had vanished from the dining room. And there were surely fewer of the ornate silver mugs that Dad had won at school? We still had Daisy, and another cow who had calved, and some laying hens, so we still had some of our own food to put on the table.

Dad rapidly put together an application for Legal Aid, based on the deposition he had sent to the MP last summer. In a few weeks he heard that aid was granted to obtain a Counsel's Opinion.

Life was becoming a nightmare of complications. The creditors meeting at the end of March gave me two months to obtain legal aid for a Counsel's Opinion on the merits of the case. The Westminster Bank told me I was overdrawn, and politely asked me not to write any more cheques. In the meantime the accountants for the creditors put me under great pressure to sell such assets as a calf and cow, in order to put some money back into the account. I protested that milk from the cow was essential to feed my family, as there was no more money coming in from sales. The accountants settled for just the sale of the calf. My family solicitor, John Ward from Robertsbridge, passed the legal case papers I had put together last year for my MP to a Mr Linden. He lived in Burwash, with a Solicitors office in London. He said that after assembling the papers, which would require some work, he hoped to obtain a Counsel's Opinion on my case in about ten days. This would probably take until about the end of May. The accountants also urgently wanted the last years hay crop sold: this had been valued at £180 for four tons. After it was collected however the dealer cavilled about the price. His first trailer load burned out due to a spark from a forest fire, and it was impossible to verify the quality of the hay. He only sent a cheque for £20. This is the result of selling under pressure to dealers; never let the farming business suspect a forced sale!

Although I had told Robin that it was alright to start at
Brighton Tec last autumn, in fact the fees for the autumn
and spring terms were still outstanding as there were
no funds. I received letters from the Bursar at Brighton
pushing me to settle or face legal action. So I wrote
putting my position to the Principal Dr Watts. He was
very sympathetic, and agreed my son's chance of A-Levels
and a career should certainly be sustained: he suggested
that I apply to the Brighton Education Committee for
an exceptional grant. As a result he was taken over by
Brighton for the summer term. He knew nothing of this.
My wife Mary received some money from her sister, and
in fact this was all that kept some food on the table.

The summer term was under way at the Tec. Dad had told me that my results
in the spring internal exams were not good enough in Pure Maths. This was a
surprise, as I had thought that my improved understanding from Mr Goodman's
lectures was carrying me through. I tried harder, and questioned every point I did
not understand. With things the way they were at the farm, I knew there would
be no more chances.

The A-Level exams came in June: I took Maths as two subjects - Pure and
Applied. As soon as I had taken the last exam, Mother said "Now you really have
to get a job. You must make a contribution to the family somehow." Most of the
students at the Tec got some sort of a summer job: I had heard of one that paid
relatively well, taking photos of holidaymakers on the promenade. So I traced the
owner of the business; he had an office over a hairdressers shop in Queens Road,
close to Brighton Station. The place reeked of ammonia and burnt paper, which
marked all ladies hairdressers; I thought the smell was already too high a price
for the hairstyles! The boss was not interested in my skills as a photographer. "It's
simple enough, we'll take you on trust. The harder thing is making a sale. The
jobs in Brighton are full. If you can get to Hastings, see my operator Jack at the
corner café opposite the White Rock theatre on the sea front." I signed a form as a
temporary worker, which covered National Insurance and tax, provided my total
earnings came under some limit.

Next day I caught the 52 bus to Hastings. It is a long trip across country, through
Brightling and Ninfield to Battle, then down to the coast and Hastings, and it took
over an hour. I had to hope that my earnings would cover the fare! The café was
a typical sea front operation, specialising in large mugs of well-urned tea, and
variations on a theme of sausage egg bacon beans and chips for between 1s 3d to
2s 6d. Jack came in, and said "Ah, the recruit. Welcome to the team!" Mostly it
was just him and me. He handed me my camera - a Leica f100 - and showed me

how to use it. "Speed 1/125 always, cloudy f5.6 , sun and clouds f8, bright sun f11. Always have the punters facing the sunlight, or sideways if it is too strong. Spend the morning with me, I'll catch the trade. You listen to the chat, and take the photos; you'll pick it up quickly enough." We went outside to the promenade. A couple of Londoners were approaching. "One of the two of you together Sir?" "This isn't my wife - don't want evidence against me!" "That's alright Sir, keep it at the office - just for a souvenir?" "Awww" Snap! "How many copies?" "Jus' the one." "Is that just for you or just for the lady?" "Awright, make it two." "Now how about one with the Pier behind you? Look, the sun's coming out again. Smiling now Madam. Tell the lady a joke Sir!" Snap!...Snap! "You'll want both of those Sir, the second one is particularly good." " When can I see them?" "We post them to you Sir, it's easier for people who are only here for the day." "But what if they're no good?" "Send them back, and we'll refund your money, or you can have other ones taken later." Jack took the man's address, and also a cool fifteen shillings. Turning to a pair of bosomy giggling girls in "Kiss Me Quick" hats he grinned "Let me have you in three different positions for seven and six my dears". I was laughing so much I had difficulty holding the camera steady. At lunch - sausage egg and chips - he counted up the takings for the morning. Fifteen pounds! "I'll book that half to each of us, as we shared the work. Now this afternoon you're on your own. Just remember, keep confident, keep smiling, and keep your temper if they are rude - some people are very rude." So I picked up my Leica, and went out and did likewise. At the end of the day I had another eight pounds of photos in the bag. I gave Jack my money and order forms. He unloaded the camera, and showed me how to put in a new film. At the end of the week I received a third of the takings as my share. I think it was about nine pounds. I subtracted my bus fares, and gave mother half the rest for my keep. I worked seven days a week for most of the summer. The trade was better at weekends, and we all needed the money. It was good fun, meeting so many people each day. But I was worn out by evening, after standing for the whole day. Hastings is a very different place from Eastbourne; it is on a fast direct railway line from London, and the town was thronged with cheap and cheerful East Enders. One wet lunchtime in the café, two women were talking to their daughters, who were late teenagers. After some heated words the girls walked huffily out. "Your Sal is a little Madam ain't she? I'd get her done if I was you - she needs taking down a peg!"

A letter for me arrived from Brighton Tec: Dr Pentland was writing to say that the Sandwich Course had been approved; did I want to apply? Did I ever! That was marvellous news. Two days later the A-Level results arrived: a couple of ticker-tape slips of paper said, on close inspection, that I had passed both Maths A-Levels, so finally I had four subjects. Brighton had offered to submit applications for us as students at the Ministry of Supply: I sent off my results and the application form that day by registered post. My father smiled: it was the first time I had seen that since last Christmas. I had no idea how bad the situation was by now.

Linden the new solicitor had encouraged me through the long wait, saying that I should not give up the fight. He was sure that I had a good case, even though the Ministry were bound to fight it. But the Counsel, who apparently handled cases for another Government department, kept putting off giving his opinion. In the meantime I was trying desperately to keep the creditors at bay, and keep the farm in some semblance of order. But there was no money even to buy materials like roof tiles, let alone to pay for labour on two-man jobs.

Finally on the 24th of August I was called up to the chambers of Mr Cornelius Penn, who happened to be an ex-Tory MP. (The Tories were still the governing party.) It was immediately clear that he had made up his mind against my case. He said in essence that, irrespective of the question of the actual nature of the disease, it would be impossible to satisfy a tribunal that it was fowl pest without actual testimony by expert witnesses to that end: indeed, many experts had already given their opinions that it was not fowl pest. (Since only Ministry staff were permitted to handle notifiable diseases, all contrary opinions were necessarily excluded!) Further, he said, the Minister was only legally required to compensate the value of stock he had ordered to be destroyed. Since no such order had been made, the Ministry had no liabilities towards my farm. Some things that he mentioned made it fairly clear that he had been discussing my case with the Ministry: he knew for instance how many blood samples had been examined back in 1950, which was not in my dossier. I consider this to have been highly unprofessional behaviour. He failed to grasp, or would not see, that my case was not simply a claim for fowl pest compensation; rather it was a claim for damages due to a conspiracy against my farm, by maladministration in not treating my case in accordance with the legal requirements from the very beginning. I was just as astonished at the behaviour of Mr Linden, my new solicitor, during this conference. Having encouraged and supported me thus far, he remained silent throughout; leaving me to argue the case myself against the Counsel, whose mind was firmly made up. They asked me to leave at the end, as they had further business to discuss. When he came out, Mr Linden said that Mr Penn was sponsoring him for an appointment as a Recorder. I did not know at the time what a Recorder was: in fact it is a signal honour for a solicitor. A Recorder becomes in effect a deputy Judge, replacing a full judge in some trials.

It was only next day that I realised what had happened. It was already obvious last year that the Vets' tactic was to keep the farm shut-down until I went out of business. Four months - rather than the predicted ten days - had now been spent to obtain the Counsel's opinion, in which time my small funds had been run down to nothing. The Counsel had certainly discussed my case with the Ministry, who had taken advantage to spin things out. The Conservative government had every interest in avoiding another scandal involving the Ministry of Agriculture, coming only two years after the Crichel Down affair, which forced the Minister to resign[1]. My solicitor had deserted me. And he was going to receive an uncommon promotion. If the farm remained empty of stock, the virus infection would eventually die out. And the Ministry would be rid of the problem without admitting their mistake. I was outraged that, despite a clear case for maladministration against them, they had dodged the issue for the second time in a year. I wrote to the Secretary of the Legal Aid office, and he decided to ask the Board for a second legal opinion with a leading counsel. The various accountants for creditors and the bank agreed to a further moratorium, provided that I agreed to assign all damages recovered to them in the first instance. John Ward, my family solicitor, told me that if I did not sign, the creditors would probably put me into bankruptcy. This would prevent me from pursuing any legal case, and put any redressment out of reach. So I signed. By October I had no funds of any kind left. I applied for National Assistance, in order to feed my family.

[1]The Crichel Down Affair was a political scandal in 1954. Before the War the Air Ministry compulsorily purchased land in Dorset for military use. In 1950 the land was transferred to the Ministry of Agriculture, who proceeded to sell it to the Crown Commissioners at a considerable profit without first offering it to the original owner, as required by law.

The Break

Ministry of Supply.
Est. 3.C.2.A.,
The Adelphi.
London W.C.2.

14th September 1956.

R.Armstrong Brown.
The Old Farm,
Cross-in-Hand,
Sussex.

I am directed to offer you an unestablished appointment in the grade of Assistant Experimental Officer in the Ministry of Supply.

1. The appointment will be at the Aeroplane and Armament Experimental Establishment, RAF Station, Boscombe Down, Amesbury, Wilts.

2. The salary at entry will be £350 x £40 annual increment. Your incremental date will be your birthday.

3. The Department will require evidence of your medical fitness to take up the appointment, to be satisfied with your references, and also to have documentary evidence of your date of birth and of the academic or technical qualifications claimed in your application form.

    ------

7. Subject to satisfactory service, you will be considered for a place on a Sandwich Course starting in early January 1957.

I am Sir,

> Your obedient servant,
> M.Crerar

I was overjoyed! I was accepted for a career that I really wanted. And at last I could reduce the burden on my parents. I had in fact been more than paying my way this summer; my best week's pay was seventeen pounds. But the photography sales were winding down now, and Jack said we would stop after next weekend. I supplied the details needed, and paid a small fee for the medical examination.

The Ministry told me to take up my appointment on a Monday morning in early October. The Ute was off the road, as there was no money for its license fee. Mr Lawson at the bungalow drove me to Heathfield Station, with one large suitcase of possessions. My parents waved me goodbye at the gate. I did not know if they would even be at the farm next January.

Salisbury

It was late afternoon when the train from Brighton slowed, and passed over a big road junction on the outskirts. An enormous Cathedral spire dominated the low buildings. From the window I could see gentle rolling hills, very much like my Downs, and beech woods turning golden in the autumn sunlight. I felt relieved: this was very like home. A taxi delivered me to Bishopsdown House in St Marks Avenue, where a bed had been reserved for me. This was a Ministry of Supply hostel for scientific staff at three research stations in the area: in fact it was like a private hotel for scientists. I was sharing a room with two others - Alastair Buck, who was about my age; and Hugh Taylor, a married draughtsman in his thirties, who went home to Ipswich at weekends. Senior staff paid a bit more and had single rooms. The place was run like an Officers Mess, and the food was very good.

In the morning Alastair accompanied me to the nearest bus stop, where we caught the red Wilts & Dorset No 3 to Amesbury. It rumbled uphill out of the city, passing a striking construction beside the road at the top of the hill. This is Old Sarum, an Iron Age fort, with a moat and a citadel, carved from the chalk of the hills. It dates from more than a thousand years before any written history in England. But I wondered what stories it could tell? Once up here, the naked grasslands of Salisbury Plain roll to the horizon in all directions. We passed a solitary inn at High Post, then after a couple of miles the bus turned right along a branch road. Along the next hill crest I now saw aircraft hangers, one of them absolutely huge, and the tail fins of aircraft. We arrived at the gates: I was going to get off, but Alastair said "No, wait." To my surprise the bus drove on past the security police into one of Britain's most secret airfields.

Boscombe Down

We got off at the next stop, and Alastair took me to the Personnel Office. "I've got a new recruit for you." Several young women looked up with varying degrees of interest. One dealt with my paperwork. I would not be paid until the end of the month; she asked if I needed an advance? I had calculated that my photography money, with care, should see me through, so I declined. She took me to see the

Training Officer, Mr Humphries, a short dark and rather fatherly person. "We have decided to place you with the Instrumentation Group. They deal with the precise calibration of aircraft instruments that are used on flight trials of new aircraft, before they are accepted for the RAF and the Navy." He took me to another low building with several wings, along a corridor, and tapped at an open office door. "This is Doug Read; he is expecting you." Doug was a genial person in his thirties, oval face, smooth brown hair, and a friendly smile. He pushed aside a magazine; reading it upside down I saw The Beekeepers Journal. He showed me the big laboratory opposite, and introduced me to my new colleagues. Derek White was a tallish good-looking man, usually with a pipe in his mouth, and unusual among scientists in that he usually wore a suit to work. Dave Trowbridge, about my age, was soldering some electronics in a box on the lab bench. Jimmy Robinson was a surprise at first, sitting on a high stool working steadily away at some measurements: Jimmy was a dwarf. But his talents were perfectly normal, and within a couple of days you soon forgot completely about the physical handicap. Jim Dolman was the watchmaker and instrument mechanic, sitting in a glass walled clean room in the corner. He could adjust an ordinary watch to keep within a second a day of GMT - a useful man to know. The laboratory itself was impressive, as it was dominated by a big vertical loop of tubing two feet in diameter, having a square section with windows at table level. This was a laboratory wind tunnel, capable of wind speeds over 100 mph. Along the walls were several altitude chambers: these were glass fronted metal boxes, connected to vacuum pumps that created air pressures equivalent to 100,000 feet altitude; they were used mainly for calibrating aircraft altimeters. We went back to the office.

Doug handed me a little pink notebook. "This is your signing-in book. Since you are an officer, you book your own times in and out. You have A-Level Science don't you? OK. Well, the immediate job is some improvements on external air thermometers. On a fast moving aircraft you cannot just stick a bulb out of the window, because you get a temperature rise due to the apparent motion of the air. We have a pitot head which brings the air velocity, even at the speed of sound, down to walking speed. Knowing the air speed, we can calculate the temperature rise, and so we deduct the rise from the measurement to get back the real air temperature. Alright so far?" I nodded. "We calibrate the probes in the lab in a little wind tunnel, where the air in the loop is cooled to −70°C in a bath of acetone with dry ice dissolved to cool it. We let it warm up slowly, and measure the platinum resistance element against a standard thermometer. You can have a go this afternoon." This was safe ground; I had done it before in the physics labs both at Eastbourne and Brighton: I was going to enjoy this. Alastair came by the lab, and we went out to the civilian canteen for lunch. Steak and kidney pie and chips with HP sauce seemed to be a standard meal - not elegant, but I was hungry!

After lunch I worked on the calibration, while Derek kept an eye on me. The little test loop made the whole place reek of acetone. Derek carefully left his pipe at the bench, as a spark could have had dramatic consequences. Safety in laboratories then depended on careful people, unlike today when it depends on draconian regulations enforced by inspectors. Alastair collected me at the end of the day, and we caught the bus back to Salisbury. "It's a fairly quiet place", he said, "until the troops get paid on Thursday evening. Then we have to watch out for ourselves through until Sunday morning." I remembered - of course! Salisbury Plain down to Dorset is covered with military camps and tank training ranges. "They are mostly National Servicemen. Once they are paid, their one idea is to come into town and get blind drunk. Then the fights start. Every evening bus out of Salisbury is followed by a Military Police Land-Rover. The MPs pick up the drunks and stop the fights; they are real toughs. By Sunday morning the squaddies are all broke with headaches - or worse - and life gets civilised again."

That night I shared a table with Dick Pattel, a very senior Scientist from Porton Down, and Dr Beryl Askew. Porton Down was home to two Ministry of Supply research stations. The Chemical Defence Experimental Establishment (CDEE) was experimenting with nerve gases developed, but fortunately not used, by Nazi Germany in the last war. The Medical Research Establishment (MRE) was working among other things on antidotes for the gas warfare chemicals from CDEE. I gathered, over supper, that a microgramme of the P agents on the skin would be fatal. With the more recent V agents a single aerosol droplet, too small even to see, would have the same result. More hair-raising even than the conversation was the calm with which they were discussed!

Workshops

I needed to get some test materials made up in the Model Workshop, a workshop staffed by a dozen skilled craftsmen for prototype fabrication. The questioning by the mechanic led to a dawning understanding that, although I was certainly well educated in physics and maths, I did not know how to do a technical drawing; and worse, I had almost no idea how machine tools worked, and what they could or could not do. How could I give instructions to these mechanics whose skills and machines I did not understand? I had a word with Doug, and with his boss George Hillier, a very practical 'hands-on' engineer. Then I went to the Training Officer with what he at first regarded as a startling request. "Can you put me in the workshop for say six weeks, like an apprentice, to be taught basic metalwork skills, and at least an introduction to machine tools? Then at least I will have a reasonable idea of what I am asking people to do." So, although instrumentation was fun, and I went back to it later, I was put under the wing of Harold, the deputy foreman of the workshop. He said, "Well, normally we take two years over this. But you've asked, and I'll be happy to go as far and as fast as you can. But you have to start at the beginning, with hand tools. So lets start with a saw; you cut out six six-inch square Dural aluminium plates, and you file them to perfect squares with a set-square." It took me a whole week, but by the end I could saw a straight line! Then I drilled and tapped and countersunk them, and screwed them together. My Box. Harold ran the rule over it and winced. "If you was an apprentice I'd say do it again. But we ain't got the time. Now we'll do the vertical power drill. You adapt the drill bit and the speed to the metal, see? And the lubricant too. Brass and copper are dead easy 'cos they're soft. Aluminium can melt and bind, breaking the drill bit. Steel is difficult, the bit must be very sharp. And stainless is a bastard - it blunts everything."

Europe and Asia

Several momentous events happened that month. The Hungarians rebelled en-masse against their Communist dictatorship, which had been installed by murder. Russia, which was bleeding Hungary white under the guise of the Comintern, knew only one response: 'class betrayal' had to be ruthlessly suppressed. Thirty thousand Hungarians fled through Austria, and arrived, mostly penniless, in the West. Although there were plenty of communists in Britain, very little was heard from the workshop agitators that month. For some reason the Russians hesitated, and started negotiating with the new Nagy government.

Then, in parallel with these events, or maybe under their cover, the Israeli Army launched a surprise attack across the Sinai desert to capture the east bank of the Suez Canal. Rapidly the British and French launched invasion forces to 're-occupy' the Canal Zone, from which they had only recently been withdrawn, 'in order to guarantee that this important lifeline for shipping remains open.', as Sir Anthony Eden said, in Churchillian vein. The Egyptians promptly sank all the ships in the southern end of the Canal, blocking it for several years. Socialists generally opposed our 'Imperialist aggression'. Conservatives like me were in favour of putting tinpot dictators like Nasser in their place. (Had we but known!) The Victor and Vulcan bombers at Boscombe Down were suddenly despatched to Cyprus - this was war. With the West in total disarray, Russian tanks suddenly rolled into Hungary, overcame the Hungarian Army, and installed a new puppet regime of communists. The Americans were outraged that Europeans should do anything without their permission; and to the total surprise of our Government, the USA banned the sale of oil or petroleum to Britain and France. Very strict petrol rationing came in immediately. Now, most boys who have grown up on a farm know how a tractor kerosine vapouriser works; and thousands of gallons of Avtur jet fuel - which is simply high quality kerosine - were standing around the airfield in drums. All it needs is an extra fuel can, a changeover valve, and a small coil of copper tube around the exhaust manifold: before the week was out several Austin Seven Specials were producing a very aromatic exhaust! Petrol was kept for starting, and for use within Salisbury city limits. Eden and company, and our country, were forced into a very humiliating climbdown. It was four decades before the world found out that the whole scenario was cooked up in secret between Ben Gurion, Eden, and the French Prime Minister. Only six people in the world knew of the plot, three Prime Ministers and their Foreign Ministers. And to think that I joined the demonstration in Salisbury Market Square in their favour!

With my first monthly pay packet in hand, and the hostel paid, I had a small margin left for a bit of a social life. I had taken my guitar, and gone down to The Two Bare Feet, a small coffee bar for the trendy-but-not-well-off set. 'My small stock-in-trade' of songs was welcome. Although I noticed that at the end of most evenings, others had their arms around the girls, while I had mine around this feminine shaped wooden box! Musing on such thoughts as I was walking home, I noticed the chestnut trees beside the path seemed to be swaying most peculiarly: not the branches - but the trunks? There were odd colours in the lights of the street lamps too. Feeling strangely weak and light headed, I wobbled back to the hostel, and fell into bed to dream wild dreams all night.

Alastair was peering at me. It must be morning, the room was in daylight. "Are you alright? You were shouting in your sleep." I tried to answer, but my tongue was stuck. I tried to get up, but the room tipped alarmingly and I fell back, weak as a kitten. "Stay there, I'll get Fanny." Mrs Fanny Banvaerts was a refugee from some previous European revolution, who tried despairingly to manage a private hotel for forty mad scientists. She looked at me, felt my forehead, and backed away quickly. "I'll get the doctor"; to Hugh and Alastair "You two don't get too near." She brought me breakfast on a tray, and put it down at the edge of my reach. When he arrived the doctor took my temperature - 105° F. He said "It was probably higher during the night. You made it anyway, if not by much. You have the Asian 'flu. You should eat if you can, and drink plenty." He prescribed aspirin and codeine to bring my temperature down, and gave the chits to Fanny, who was looking through the doorway. "You will be off work for at least two weeks."

I think it was longer. I just lay in bed, my legs hardly strong enough to carry me to the toilet and back. While I was lying there, barely capable of reading John Wyndham's 'The Day of the Triffids', I heard a news-flash on the BBC on Hugh's radio. The Russians had launched Sputnik 1: the idiot bleeping of its telemetry radio circled the world every ninety minutes like an orbiting child's toy. The Americans gnashed their teeth in frustration, as their own Vanguard project had blown-up on the launch pad only weeks previously. And here was one of the essential ingredients of Wyndham's nightmare, a military satellite, cheeping like a day-old chick over our heads!

Machines

"Hello stranger, we wondered if you'd left us?" Harold looked at my pale face, and passed me a cup of workshop tea so strong the spoon almost stood up in it. "I think it may have been a bit close, actually." He looked at me strangely. "There'll be a few as won't be coming back" he said, "young 'uns too. Still, and seein' as here you are, we'll go on with the learnin'." Before I left at Christmas, I could turn steel on a lathe, and even cut screw threads. I could machine profiles on a vertical milling machine; and I could harden machine steel, then grind it to a precision of 2/10,000ths of an inch on a horizontal diamond wheel grinder. I was shown how to get extraordinarily precise measurements using a clock gauge standing on the machine bed. Mr Humphries looked in every week or so, to check on progress. At the end he told me "When we get scientists they usually come from University, and leave the practical stuff to the engineers and technicians. But being able to do the lot is a great idea. I am proposing this to the Ministry, so they start all their applied science studentships this way." I felt pleased; this was a feather in my cap before the course-work had even begun! Harold said "Even if you do have a funny accent, I seldom had anyone who got his hands dirtier or picked things up faster than you. Pity about the other twenty one months - I could've made an engineer out of you!" He winked, and shook my hand.

I got a lift all the way back to Mayfield Flat with Johnny Johnson, an Experimental Officer on electronics trials. I managed to get home with another lift to Cross-in-Hand, and I carried my suitcase back to the farm from there. Everyone was relieved to see me: Mother pressed a mug of hot elderberry cordial into my hand. It tasted good.

The Farm That Wasn't

When I left in October, I did not know if the family would still be here at Christmas. Well, physically they were still here, and that was a relief, though I had no idea how they had done it. But apart from Pixie and about two dozen surviving chickens, they were the only living beings on the farm. The cow and the calf had been sold under pressure from the accountants. I had been there when poor old Daisy, who had been dry for two years, climbed into the knackers lorry; puzzled, but trusting to the last. The last loads of hay, which could have kept Pixie through a hard winter had, also under pressure from the accountants, been trucked away by an agent who reneged on the payment. Rather than leave her pony with just frosty grass for forage, Nonie, helped by Mum, had been climbing over the wall of the Marchands (ex Oakes) farm vegetable garden, scrumping winter greens through the worst of the winter. It was Diana Marchand who had taught Nonie to ride several years previously: but now the farm was abandoned. I confess I have no memories of that Christmas. Possibly it is just as well.

Regrets

The Law Society
South Eastern Legal
Aid Area

2nd January 1957.

Mr W.H.Armstrong Brown.
The Old Farm.
Cross-in-Hand.

Dear Sir,

I have received your letter of 28th December, and enclosures, which I now return.

Your application for authority to instruct two Counsel limited to obtaining the opinion of Leading Counsel was duly considered by my Committee at their meeting yesterday, and I regret that the application was refused. Your solicitors have been notified accordingly.

Yours faithfully,

C.A.Potter. Area Secretary.

Dad left early one winter morning, riding his old black bike. He was carrying his battered carpentry case, that he had made himself as a schoolboy. Mum hesitantly told us that he had started working for Charlie Vidal, who had a local Landscape Gardening business. "Otherwise, there will be nothing to eat." She smiled bravely, but the look in her eyes was bitter.

Brighton

The 18 bus seemed unusually muted on that first day of the new term. The younger girls at the back were very quiet. I said something about it to Nonie.

"Oh, you didn't know about Rosalind MacDonald?" Alastair MacDonald was a contemporary of mine at Eastbourne; Boofy was his little sister, aged about twelve. "No, what about her?" "She died. Just before Christmas. Asian flu'." I remembered what Harold had said, back at Boscombe Down. She was a lovely kid. I was horrified.

At the Tec the members of the new Sandwich Course assembled for the first time. There were eight of us. Peter Forte I already knew from Boscombe Down, and the weekly Land-Rover trip down to Bournemouth Tec. We had George Moore and John Ingham from English Electric in Liverpool, Janet Kent from an armaments establishment, Mark Dawe from The Ministry in Christchurch, Mick Martin from the Metal Box Co in Crawley, and Jim Gregg from Winfrith in Dorset. Peter and I knew our way around Brighton already, but the others were on the ball, and had already found 'digs'. Our funds were cut back from £7 a week salary to a £5 weekly grant. I lived at the farm, with a student bus-pass renewed by the generous county education office. I gave Mum half my grant: I had been better-off as a prom photographer! There was no money to throw around. For my father, there was no money at all - period.

The Tec minced few words: "We are setting our sights on honours degree standard for this course, above an ordinary BSc or Higher National Diploma. We are calling it a College Diploma for now, but we hope to get it accepted nationally. You will have to do three academic years work in four six month periods over four years. The standard will be high, we will go fast, and you will have to keep up. There will be a lot of written preparation every evening, so don't plan for much of a social life." Dr Pentland looked round with his smile which was not really a smile, and closed his folder firmly.

It was as he said. Living out in the country, any social life was difficult, though not impossible, as it turned out. There was a small social group called the Hobbies Club, run by Mrs Swann in Heathfield for teenagers - which I still was. And sometimes I had a few shillings left to go to the Saturday dance at the State Hall. I walked a few girls home afterwards, though girls were fairly reserved in those days. But it was at one of those dances that I was asked by a bright young woman to come across to a table. A few young people of my age said "We are from the Hailsham Young Conservatives, and we are looking around to see if there are enough people to form a branch here in Heathfield. We are mostly a social organisation. We only get a bit political to help in General Elections. But apart from that we hold social events, go on visits, organise dances, and generally make friends." I left them my name and address, and soon afterwards got an invitation to the inaugural meeting. After introductions, we were left to organise a committee, and vote it into office. Sally Mathews, a live wire who worked at the

High Street jewellers, became Chairman. Maybe because of my self assurance - now improved by prom photography! - I was her assistant. Next week she said "I have been trying to call you all week, but your phone is always out of service?" I asked Mum: "Well, we can't pay the phone bill. In the end they seem to have cut us off." I told Sally there was damage somewhere on the line: wisely she didn't press the subject.

The Secretary,
The Law Society,
No2 Legal Aid Area

4. February. 1957.

Dear Sir,

(para 3) Further I received a letter from Mr Linden on the 13 Dec, in which he stated that my farm should not in his opinion be sold as a Poultry Farm, or indeed as a farm suitable for Poultry. That, in his opinion would be a misrepresentation. He stated "I would go further and say that in my opinion when offering the farm for sale you should expressly say that it is not suitable for poultry." I have no doubt at all that this would suit the Ministry very well indeed, but should not I and my solicitor consider the interests of creditors?

I am extremely grateful to you for your help, and trust that I may still obtain satisfaction in this matter; and above all at least ventilation of these thoroughly disgraceful matters which reflect very little credit on otherwise honourable professions.

Yours sincerely,

W.H.Armstrong Brown.

Dad had spent so much effort on trying to obtain justice that he had let letters from accountants, and even Income Tax demands and Rates, go unanswered. He had made no money; he had lost his farm, and so how could he be taxed? Rates however have a prior claim on everything. Dad continued to fight even while his ship was sinking. He took our case to the Labour party: they were interested at first, but then apparently accepted the Ministry's quiet assurances that Dad had an obsession about fowl pest. He made the case to the newspaper The People. They found the story scandalous and completely convincing. But they decided regretfully that it could not be published without naming names, and that those named would sue for libel with all the weight and funds of the Ministry to back them. Unhappily, The People decided it could not afford to publish my father's story.

There was a further creditors meeting shortly after the Legal Aid door was closed. They kept to their position, that in the circumstances it would only waste further money making my father bankrupt. It had the advantage that Dad was still free to pursue his legal action, if he found a way to do so. The solicitor Linden advised for bankruptcy, in spite of the creditors' decision. But if a debtor avoids bankruptcy, the debts remain. Twenty years later, he was still working to pay them off.

The End

The 'For Sale' notice was there by the garden gate when I cycled downhill from the Brighton bus one evening. I knew it had to happen, but when I saw it I started crying inside, silently and tearlessly. It must have been at the end of March. We were all silent. It was the death sentence on our home. How my parents felt I dare not think, even today.

Sometime in the spring I know there was an offer of £3800 from a pig farmer for the farm. My father was incensed; a few years earlier it had been valued at £12000 as a going concern. The financial world battens on forced sales. In May Mum told us the bank had accepted an even lower offer, in order to close the affair. We had until the end of July to leave. The hard work at the Tec helped take my mind off the situation. Nothing helped my father. When he came home from his labouring job, he sat in his armchair, staring blankly at the wall.

There were first year exams in mid July. I must have passed, but I have no memory of it now. It was a relief not to be at home; but every time I thought of it, the gaping void inside me opened again

I packed all my possessions in my school trunk. Everything had to go this time, including my bike and the guitar. "How am I going to get these to the station, Dad?" The Ute was still off the road, without a license disc. "You had better go over and ask Ted Stevens, next house to Jupp's bakery. I think he still does carting." Dad's voice was listless and bitter. I walked across Woodfield, down Warren Lane to the bakery and the next-door twin cottages, and knocked on the door. He was sitting at the table, and didn't ask me in. "Can you do a job for me tomorrow? I have a big trunk and some things, to catch the 12.15 train." "What's wrong with your Dad's van then?" Ted was no great friend of my father, having been a familiar of Bumper in past years. "The gearbox is broken" I lied. He looked me in the eyes, opened his mouth to say something, then shut it again. "Alright, about eleven thirty be okay?" On the way back I saw a man, just sitting on the Longfield style, simply looking at the farm. I knew it was Mr Field, the new owner. I tried to hate him, but I couldn't. I suddenly realised it was already his farm, not ours.

Next morning I packed the last things, and we got them down to the front door. Then I went out for a last look at everything. I walked across to Possingworth Park. The Nissen huts had all gone, and on their bases beside the loop of army roads a couple of new houses were in construction. I closed my eyes, and tried to see the cedar trees where Nonie and I had learned to climb, and to see again that amazing sunset when the sky caught fire. But the pictures would not come, all I could see was the mess around me. I walked to the top of the farm, up in D field beside the Fir Grove. The woods and the Downs, even Pevensey Bay, all were still there along the horizons. This place, and this view which had been mine all my life, were no longer mine. There was a drumming of hooves, and Nonie appeared, riding Pixie. She looked at me, then round at the view. We said nothing - words couldn't say what we were feeling. Unusually, there was a southeast wind: the oast-house cowl was pointing towards the park - inland - to London, and away. I tried to feel angry: I even tried to cry. But there was nothing inside me but a numb and dry-eyed emptiness.

Ted's battered green truck pulled up at the gate. We loaded the trunk and the bike into the back. Ted roped them down. The family had only five days left before they had to leave. They had nowhere to go. I can only remember my mother being there to see me off. "I hate leaving you like this, but I can't see what I can do to help." Through now-filling eyes I saw her smile bravely at me. "Don't worry about us, we'll find something. But you have a job to do. You have to be our success story for now. We'll be alright. And remember - Do Thy Damnedest!"

The old truck ground noisily away up the hill. I did not trust myself to look back. You only have one birthplace, one home. Losing mine hurt so much that it was almost thirty years before I could bear to look at it again.

Paradise Lost

EPILOGUE

After The End

I set out to write the story of my youth, and my growing up on a farm in Sussex. You have only one childhood. Farm children are taught to work, gently at first. They know from the beginning that the butter they churn, the eggs they collect, are valued; their contribution may be small, but it is real. Amazingly perhaps, all of us, who were the children in these tales, look back on our lives there as happy years. We had a loving home and family, we all had our own friends, and we had the fields and the woods to play in freely. We loved the wildlife, the rabbits, the foxes and the hawks, the carpets of primroses, bluebells and cowslips in the springtime woods, the clover and watermint in the summer, the wild rose, the wild hops, and the fruits of the autumn all around us. Daisy and Pixie were characters - they were our friends. The end was almost unbelievably bitter, and maybe it hardened all of us.

When I discussed this story with Penny, who is doing the illustrations, she said "You cannot possibly just leave the story there. You had gone, but we remained behind. And it wasn't the end."

I never knew exactly what happened until a few days ago. Nonie said " I had been giving riding lessons on Pixie to various schoolfriends from Lewes, in order to earn a little money to buy some fresh horseshoes. After you left, time was running out. I knew I couldn't keep Pixie. Next afternoon I rode her down to Waldron, and gave her to one of my riding pupils, Jennifer Allen. The Allens had a smallholding, and Jennifer would love Pixie just as I did. I had already left Lewes Grammar School. As I walked back to the farm, I knew that Dad would be sitting blankly in his chair. And I knew that Mum would not dare leave him alone. I think I just grew up in that minute, that afternoon. I thought 'It's up to me then.' I had an idea. Angela Simpson had also taken some riding lessons with me. Her mother had taken us a

Bluebell

few times over to her own father's place at Brockwood, near Burwash, for picnics. He had a new bungalow in the grounds; but their old family house was standing there, empty and a bit dilapidated, but still habitable. I asked Mrs Simpson if we could use it, if possible for free, against caring for it. She checked: Grandpa Rix said we were welcome if we just paid for the rates and the services we used. I took Penny over there on our bikes. We worked for several days to clean the place up. And we moved in."

The first letter I received from Mum afterwards was addressed from Brockwood, and said Mrs Simpson had arranged it for us. That was only partly true.

The Long Road Home.

Although I had left home, as Penny said, the tale did not simply end there. Living at Brockwood was not unpleasant in summer, but it was drafty and bitterly cold in winter. My father was still working as a carpenter on Vidal's landscape gardening team. Patrick once found our mother in tears; she had to pawn her rings to pay for the rates. "Don't let Dad know – it would break his heart." Nonie, denied the possibility of A levels, had few career possibilities. She left in the first winter to start her nursing studies. Life at Brockwood continued for one and a half years, until Dad was taken on as a poultryman in London Colney by a farmer who was an arrogant J.P.. After six months he was fired - for looking annoyed when summoned from his bed at 6 a.m. on a Sunday, to re-assure the paranoid owner that he had in fact locked the hen houses the previous night! He found a temporary carpenter's job to pay the rent on his tied cottage, until he landed a better job in the Cotswolds, to set up and manage a large intensive poultry unit on a big farm. Nonie's savings paid for the move. The hours were long and the pay low, but a pleasant flat in a large manor house went with it. Mum went out to work as a cook to help make ends meet. Penny succeeded at her A levels, and went to Weymouth to study teaching. I could sometimes meet her, as by then I was working in Christchurch. But Dad was worried about the management of this farm: so he found a job to set up and manage a turkey breeding unit on a large farm in Leicestershire. The salary was still low, but a car was provided. I thought things were looking up, until I saw he was having to start a big diesel generator in mid-winter by hand! His physique became just skin and bone; but he made a joke of being nicknamed 'Oxfam'

Then I had a phone call from Dad: my mother had suffered a stroke. At first he had thought she was imagining it, and sent her off to have a hot bath - her one daily luxury. The doctor told him later that it may have saved her life; but as a treatment it was so drastic that no doctor would dare to prescribe it! However, she was permanently weakened on one side. Nonie wanted to go home and nurse her, but Mum would not hear of it. Over the years the turkey farm became a growing success. The farm owner recognised Dad's worth; and he was bought a new bungalow, to be repaid over a five years interest-free loan out of the production bonuses that Dad negotiated. A return visit to Sussex may have come to the notice of the farm creditors. Dad was sued over the debts; we children contributed to help pay them, until our parents asked us not to, as our own families were coming along. Patrick took A levels, and started at Southampton University. Relations with the farm manager became strained: it transpired that the turkey farm - now running on four different sites – was in fact paying for the losses of the parent farm. Then the blow fell. When Dad suspected that the manager and the senior foreman were running a scam on the farm accounts, he was suddenly fired with little notice while still six months short of his pension. Suddenly, out of the blue, he was offered a post as a manager with Attleborough Turkeys in Norfolk, who had been impressed with his results. This became the reward for a very hard life. He was well paid; but better, his work was at last valued at its true worth. He worked full time until he was over seventy, then slowly cut back, and he retired at last aged seventy seven. Mother looked after him devotedly. The debts, into which they had been pushed by an outrageous conspiracy, were finally repaid.

During those years they could enjoy visiting their children and a tribe of grandchildren, both in England and abroad. We were sitting on a headland looking over the Aegean one evening: Mother said "When I had that stroke I thought my life was over. If only I had known how much there was still to live for, places to see, and your families to watch growing, it would have made such a difference, and been so much easier to bear."

When our mother's health declined, and he could no longer care for her at home, Dad visited her every day in the Wayland Hospital for four years. After her death, he continued visiting the lonely amputees in the hospital, bringing them fruits from his own garden. Patrick and Celia often cared for him when his own health started to fail.

I once asked him if he hated Sussex, where he had been so badly wronged? He said "No. I love that beautiful county. The sun is warmer there: the wind is softer, even the shine on the leaves is brighter there. I love it like nowhere else in England. Only….. I can't go back." But he did – once. He went back, and at their favourite picnic spot above Cuckmere Haven he sprinkled our mother's ashes on the short Downland turf. Some years later Nonie took his ashes to join hers. We only heard at his funeral that in Attleborough he was known to the whole neighbourhood as 'the nice man'.

Looking Back

Penny said "My life has not been very easy either. But if I have learned one thing, it is this. It is useless and harmful to cherish your hurts. You have to look for the positive, everywhere. What amazes me, looking back, is how much our parents achieved, given the appalling situation that they were in. Dad was broken from being a farm-owner to being a jobbing labourer, in debt for more than his prospective life earnings. But through the long and humiliating climb-back to management of big farms and gratitude from their owners, he and Mum kept us together as a family until we could fend for ourselves. They saw all of us through into Higher Education. You went to the Tec and qualified in your field. Nonie qualified as a State Registered Nurse. She once wrote home "I would never have believed I could love anything as much I love nursing." I went to Training College and became a teacher, which was what I always wanted. As for Patrick, although it was a long slog through some poor schools, he went to University and became an engineer. And Mum went out in winter to cook in Transport Cafes high in the Cotswolds, to help Dad earn enough to keep us. They were heroes. Their real achievement - was us."

Wild Rose

Wherefore praise we famous men,
From whose bays we borrow.
They that put aside today
All the joys of their today,
And with toil of their today -
Bought for us tomorrow.

From Stalky & Co. Rudyard Kipling.

Robin Armstrong Brown grew up on a farm in East Sussex. He studied first at Eastbourne College, then at Brighton Technical College, where he got a degree in Applied Physics. He worked for the Ministry of Supply on scientific instrumentation.

He later moved to Geneva, where he met his wife Diana. With their daughters Susie and Amanda they enjoyed skiing in the mountains and sailing on the lakes, founding a folksong club, and singing and dancing on the amateur stage. Robin worked for the rest of his career at CERN, the European accelerator laboratory, and gained a doctorate for his early research there. He managed several large systems projects, and rose to be a Senior Physicist. Susie followed her father, gained a doctorate in life sciences, and now works for the RSPB; Amanda gained her Articles as a solicitor and worked in investment banking before becoming a full-time mother to her three children.

Before retirement, at Di's prompting, they sold their lake yacht and bought a Swedish ocean-going yacht. Together they have sailed around Europe from Sweden to Turkey, crossed the Atlantic to Brazil, and are now sailing right round the Caribbean. When not sailing they live in France near Geneva. Robin still keeps up his minstrel routine at barbecues and camp fires, given the slightest excuse! He has written a number of magazine articles about the cruising life. This is his first full length book.

Contact: robin@thefarmersboy.info

Printed in Great Britain
by Amazon